CONVERSATIONS ON MODERNISM

CONVERSATIONS ON MODERNISM

SUKRITA PAUL KUMAR

Vani Book Company

Vani Book Company

Head Office

4695, 21-A, Daryaganj, New Delhi 110 002, India
Phone +91 11 23273167 Fax : +91 11 23275710

Registered Bookstores and Offices

Ashok Rajpath, Patna 800 004, Bihar
Coffee House Campus, Mahatma Gandhi Marg, Allahabad 211 001, Uttar Pradesh
Mahatma Gandhi International Hindi University, Wardha 442 001, Maharashtra
Sultania Road, Motia Park , Bhopal 462 001, Madhya Pradesh
Goripur Taliya Para, 313, R.B.C. Road 24- Parganas (North) Kolkata 743 166, West Bengal

www.vaniprakashan.com
marketing@vaniprakashan.in
sales@vaniprakashan.in

CONVERSATIONS ON MODERNISM
by Sukrita Paul Kumar

ISBN : 978-93-89915-24-2
Non-Fiction/Interviews

First Edition 2020

Price : ₹ 399

Printed and bound in India at City Press, Delhi-110 095

Vani Prakashan's signature motif is created by Artist Maqbool Fida Husain

Tales
of
creation
emerge
through the
wrinkled clouds
of the nightly
coal skies,
Streaks of lightning
display undefined woes
and cheer
dripping from
time gone
and one
yet to come

Sukrita

CONTENTS

Acknowledgements

My thanks to the Indian Institute of Advanced Study, Shimla, for the facilities granted to me to conduct the dialogues collected in this book during my tenure as a Fellow there. Thanks to IIAS for awarding the fellowship to me to work on modernism in Hindi and Urdu short fiction.

I evolved the critical strategy of holding 'dialogues' with eminent authors, critics and philosophers as one of the ways to get greater insight into my research area. I am thankful to IIAS for publishing these dialogues earlier. My books *The New Story* and *Breakthrough* were also published by IIAS as companion volumes to these Conversations.

I wish to acknowledge the following journals in which some of these dialogues were published: *Indian Literature,* New Delhi; *Urdu Canada,* Canada; *The New Quest,* Pune; *The Hindu, Patriot,* Delhi; *India International Centre Quarterly,* Delhi.

Most of all, I am grateful to the writers, critics and philosophers who spared long hours for these discussions.

For the re-publication of this book by Vani Book Company, I am thankful to Aditi Maheshwari of Vani Book Company, and then to Urvashi Vashist who helped me edit the conversations.

Preface

The questions on literary modernism, raised over three decades ago when I was a Fellow at the Indian Institute of Advanced Study, seem as relevant today as they were then. They were issues that had compelled me to reach out to the stalwarts whose voices are present in this volume. Unfortunately, many of them are no more now. Such writers and critics as Qurratulain Hyder, Nirmal Verma, Wazir Agha, Ramesh Chandra Shah, Jeelani Bano, Namwar Singh, Joginder Paul, Muhammad Ali Siddiqui, Kathleen Raine and philosophers such as Margaret Chatterjee and M.M. Agrawal, were at their creative zenith at the time when I sought them out for responses. Some of these issues were niggling within me while I was working on modernism in Hindi and Urdu short story at the Institute in Shimla. The two writers from Pakistan, Wazir Agha from Lahore and Muhammad Ali Siddiqui from Karachi were very gracious in giving me their precious time while on their short visits to Delhi at different points of time. Kathleen Raine too generously offered to speak to me when she came to India in the late eighties. It was my good fortune that I was able to meet all these writers and also record their voices! Even though many of them are no longer present today, their perspectives recorded here act as beacon lights for us to traverse the domain of modernism in our literary culture.

I believe these conversations help create a better understanding of 'the new story' (*Nayi Kahani* and *Naya Afsana*) in

Hindi and Urdu amongst the scholars and readers of literature. I must point out here that the valuable insights yielded by these dialogues eventually led to my book on the subject of modernism. What evolves as the "new" in each age is indeed, both unique as also, a realization of what is actually 'dynamic' in some underlying currents of tradition!

This book of conversations now comes in its new avatar, thanks to Vani Book Company, if only to re-kindle the debates of yester years, so pertinent and relevant for a meaningful engagement with the literature of present times too. The continuities, confluences as also ruptures in the flow of literary movements need to be discerned as relational with the past, specially since 'modernism' emerged as a powerful fountainhead for what was to come in future.

A significant addition in this book of Conversations is a narration of some of my interactions with the eminent writer Krishna Sobti, culled out of the series of her dialogues with me, recorded over a period of about three years before she passed on in January 2019. The inclusion of her voice in this volume seemed pertinent to me as that of one with a powerful progressive presence in literature in India, contemporary with the Hindi and Urdu writers included here.

Sukrita Paul Kumar

July 15, 2019

Introduction

Understanding 'modern' Hindi and Urdu fiction means understanding the interface of the writer of '*Nayi Kahani*' or "*Naya Afsana*" (new story) with the reality of the 60's and 70's of the twentieth century India. The post-Independence/ post-Partition life experience compelled a fresh creative articulation in the changed socio-political environs. Writers projected their capability of at once experiencing reality as well as stepping outside it to understand, assess, and locate new forms to express and define the new reality. Twentieth century literature from all over the world in fact presented a whole range of new forms and styles through which the writer chose to delineate and capture the changing realities. The traditional, apparently straight-jacketed forms seemed inadequate to contain the broad and complex spectrum of human experience: new vistas opened through an intensely philosophic and psychological probing into human existence and its place in the universe. Modernism, a rather elusive concept, emerged as a blanket term, a convenient label to describe the new dynamics of human consciousness.

Mid-twentieth century Hindi and Urdu fiction seems to evince some of the same preoccupations, strategies, and stylistic choices as did literature in early-twentieth century Europe. There seemed to be a distinct and deliberate divergence from 'tradition' accompanied by a social disruption, an awareness of emptiness, a general loss of individual identity, and an experience of loneliness and estrangement. A scan of the post-Independence Urdu and Hindi short story demonstrates a heightened questioning of values, disillusionment, and what may be termed as 'modern temper' tinged with some cynicism. It is precisely this body of literary work that has inspired these dialogues in the present volume. As the reader approaches the individual artist's imagination through her or his fiction, it becomes increasingly necessary to comprehend the sensibility which actually produced that work.

The following dialogues with eminent writers of modern Hindi and Urdu short fiction, critics and philosophers, were undertaken to place and interpret modern Urdu and Hindi fiction within a larger, global, social and artistic framework. The intention is to strive and define the artistic climate of Indian modernism as a backdrop to the critical and philosophical approaches to these literatures. In these conversations there is an attempt to make the writers step out of their work and consider themselves the product of a specific culture. At times, they return to their original state of creative adventures while recalling the creative process. Whereas celebrated writers in the west have developed defences and they acquire public personae that allow for little spontaneous interaction, the Indian writer – fortunately is far more accessible. Unguarded and unpretentious dialogue with them is more forthcoming, making the exercise meaningful, unpredictable as well as enjoyable. Indeed, the dynamism of the dialogue depends on the undercurrent of mutual understanding and the responsiveness of those in conversation. Just as writers dispensed with the private lines beyond which they would not usually articulate their process of writing, the interviewer acted as appreciative audience, impartial witness, and at times even as critical authority as the need arose, sometimes remaining in the background as a quiet presence merely ensuring the continuity of communication. The questioning needed to be both incisive and receptive.

Since the term 'modern' designates a distinctive kind of imagination expressed through specific themes and literary forms, I have sought in every interview to newly understand the concept with each distinctive mind. The breadth of intention and style perceived in modern Hindi and Urdu writing awaits a comprehensive analysis for a definition of modernity and modernism that may be arrived at. The modern, which is at once immediate and obscure, intimate and elusive, is not merely a chronological description. Though intellectual and philosophical explorations of modernism have been attempted, an objective examination of literary modernism seems to have been evaded for a long time. Particularly in the Indian context, even though a shift in sensibility is easily discernible, adequate critical analysis of the phenomenon is missing. Does literary Hindi and Urdu modernism project indigenous, authentically Indian concerns or does it dominantly reflect Euro-centric modernisms? Since modernism implies a kind of disinheritance, does the vacuum get filled with alien concepts and values? How much of the experiential quality of modern Indian literature smack of western influence? Can we evolve a definition of modernism which is strictly and convincingly descriptive of the Indian reality? These are some of the intriguing questions raised in the ensuing discussions. The purpose is exploratory. There is no attempt to argue a specific theory of modernism. However, some insights that emerge in these dialogues may help to design some theoretical premises.

The vociferous voice of the eminent Urdu writer Qurratulain Hyder clearly blames critics for not demonstrating genuine concern for literary works, and as the Hindi writer Nirmal Verma too points out, there is a dearth of critical feedback or intellectual stimulation for the modern Indian writer. Jeelani Bano, who also writes in Urdu, takes a similar stance against the critical climate characterized by complacence; she particularly criticizes the "awards culture" and the consequent politicking in Urdu literary circles. What seems to emerge then is that the modern Indian writer tends to be particularly self-conscious about being in an insular world. In these conversations then, ranging from momentary crystallization of responses to ideas and beliefs, statements of these writers are testimony to what kind of minds are at work, at once creating and responding to reality and imaginative situations.

Nirmal Verma recommends that specific distinctions be made by the critic between, say, the loneliness in a tradition-ridden Indian society where families are beginning to break, and the loneliness in a so called 'liberated' individuated western society. Naive comparisons do not help to evolve the understanding of a distinctive Indian modernism/s. A matter of great concern, notes Verma, is the lack of even a mechanical critical cognition of the past in Indian writing. "We are living," he says, "without any mythological past." This focuses attention on an important distinguishing feature: the literary modernism of Yeats and Eliot creates a nostalgia for the past through a dominant literary use of myth and history.

A discussion on the creative process with one of Urdu's major writers, Joginder Paul, unravels the modern writer's liberation from traditional constraints that a literary form may impose on the creative imagination. His sharp awareness of the limits of 'freedom' for the writer, and his utmost commitment to the authentic representation of a creative experience projects the modern writer's sensitivity to the question of genuineness of artistic expression. Talking about the literary form, Kathleen Raine says, "Form, in reality proceeds from life itself, as in the form of a plant; it grows from life itself." The creative process then, to a modern writer, denotes a discovery of the artist's own form and style, through an essential contact with the perceived reality of experience.

Wazir Agha, a critic and also himself an important poet in Urdu, makes a very valid point when he talks about the easy cross-fertilization of ideas between the east and the west in the modern world. An awareness of alienation then, as he says, is not the monopoly of the west or that loneliness cannot be a feature of merely urban literature. About the same question, Mohammed Ali Siddiqui, a distinguished critic in Urdu from Pakistan, maintains that some of the modeers in both India and Pakistan have been able to absorb western modernism and readjust it in accordance to the local context, while some are quite medieval and obscurantist. He criticizes what he calls glamorization of certain notions and romanticization of fetishized artefacts: say, for instance, the bullock cart. This kind of nostalgia according to him retards progress or futuristic thinking. Indeed, to propound theories of what modernism is may stifle the rather open, many-layered consciousness of the creative writer. Siddiqui would rather not create any definitions which might limit the scope and diversity of the concept of modernism.

It is in such a context that Ramesh Chandra Shah's perceptive comment about the modern mind having discovered the value of the pagan and developed a pluralistic sensibility acquires a particular relevance. What Nietzsche and Marx did to the western psyche, he remarks, Gandhi and Sri Aurobindo did in the Indian situation, as shapers of modern Indian psyche. However, the lack of *swaraj* in ideas, a failure to confront and define the Indian situation and the tendency to locate solutions in alien cultures, makes literary modernism too literary in India. He quotes the names of some modern Hindi writers who appear as "modern men in search of a soul" and those who try to give evidence of ingenuity through their creative ventures.

Namwar Singh looks at 'modernism' as an experience of reaction, acceptance, and rejection of the transformation of sensibility. He qualifies the modernism of the late thirties in India as less of an experience and more of an intellectual exercise which seeped into Indian culture gradually and evolved into a real experience much after Independence.

It is interesting to note the differences between the two philosophers Margaret Chatterjee and M.M. Agrawal in this volume, in their answers to the questions raised. Margaret Chatterjee recognizes how cosmopolitanism is built into what might be called 'modern'. She looks askance at those who continue to talk of tradition and put the clock back politically, socially, and in other ways in the name of Indianness. She connects this with xenophobia and calls this feature "anti-modern" and believes that modernism amongst the fanatic traditionalists is a mere veneer. M.M. Agrawal, on the other hand, traces the emergence of modern values and fresh concerns in the Indian society from the very beginning of the twentieth century. He refers to the late nineteenth century/ early twentieth century Indian Renaissance as a period of Enlightenment and shows how an axiological revolution took place then, bringing about a change in the social structure of the country. Secular ideas, rational thought, and scientific outlook got injected into the national bloodstream then. Establishing a love-hate relationship between tradition and modernity, he shows how modernity draws its justification from the very past it seems to be rejecting. Since the moral authority sought to justify new ideas and fresh values, modernity gets assimilated and indigenized while relating to the Indian past.

This volume presents a valuable addition to the list of writers in conversations – that of the eminent Hindi writer Krishna Sobti. It is my good fortune that I had been in an on-going dialogue with Krishna Sobti over a number of years towards the end of her life. Even though there was no organized dialogue with her on modernism as such, I decided to include her voice in this volume, primarily because she was a formidable contemporary of the writers in this book and her ample contribution to "modern fiction" in Hindi facilitates the understanding of the modern temper in Indian literature. The autonomy she cherished for herself gets reflected in her pulsating characters, each of whom carves out her own destiny, be it Mitro of *Mitro Marjani*, Mehak of *Dilo Danish* or the mother of *Ay Ladki*.

These discussions with writers, critics, and philosophers demonstrate how specific interrogation may transform into a collective conversation. The interviewer has tried to retain the dynamism of the exchange of ideas alongside presenting a faithful transcription. Further, the mode of questioning and the direction of the discourse depended largely on the interviewer's understanding of the writings of the interviewed writers. Third, since modernism and the representation of the modern stance in literature are fused into each other, the philosopher's or the critic's perceptions are as illuminating as those of the writers. And finally, these interviews attempt to record the voice, the thinking voice, of those interviewed. This voice is oftentimes different from that heard in their written words. The spoken word offers a dimension of expression that may not be available in writing. These conversations were held in Urdu, Hindi or/and English to maintain the comfort level of the interviewees. The translation into English was done soon after, and each text produced was approved by the interviewee for publication.

Qurratulain Hyder

On the Modern Short Story and the Critic in Urdu

QURRATULAIN HYDER

Padma Bhushan Qurratulain Hyder (1927-2007) was without question the grand 'modern' dame of post-independence Urdu writing. She was honoured with the Jnanpith Award and the Sahitya Akademi Fellowship. She received the Sahitya Akademi Award for her short story collection Patjhar ki Awaz. *Her magnum opus* Aag ka Darya, *an extraordinary telling of subcontinental history and an enactment on the action of time itself, was translated into fourteen languages by the National Book Trust. She herself "recreated" the novel in English forty years after its original 1959 Urdu publication. Educated in India and abroad, Hyder was associated in various important capacities with publications such as the* Daily Telegraph, *London,* The Imprint, *Bombay, and* The Illustrated Weekly of India. *She also served as broadcaster for the Urdu Services of the B.B.C. and as Adviser to the Chairman, Central Board of Film Censors. A Visiting Professor at Aligarh Muslim University and Professor Emeritus, Khan Abdul Gaffar Khan Chair at Jamia Millia Islamia, she lectured extensively at the Universities of Chicago, Texas, California, and Arizona, and she served as resident for the University of Iowa's International Writing Program. Her work is compared in scope with that of Gabriel Garcia Marquez; her influence on Indian modernism has been profound, and she is much celebrated for her contribution to Urdu literature.*

SUKRITA: Philosophers and literary critics have expended many words on the "loneliness" of a creative artist. I would like to begin our discussion with the peculiar sense of loneliness that you may have encountered as a woman creative writer, writing in Urdu in India. Have you been conscious of being situated at an uncommon intersection that may have caused a discomfort to you as a writer? Or has that been a position of privilege? Do you have any specific experiences related to loneliness?

QURRATULAIN HYDER: You have asked three questions; one is regarding the loneliness of the creative writer. This may sound rather pompous but let's face it, it is very much there. It has always been there, with any artist anywhere in the world. A writer writes in isolation. The loneliness of a western writer is framed sociologically, but we are not concerned with that now. You have another point - the loneliness of a woman writer. Well, a woman writer, whether in the west or here in the east is more or less in an identical position. And then, to accentuate it further you speak of the loneliness of a woman writer of Urdu. That loads the question, and to top it all, a woman writer's loneliness writing in Urdu in India!

Ah well, perhaps it is not really all that bad! Writing in Urdu in India makes no difference – writing in Urdu in Canada, Pakistan or anywhere else, according to me, would not change the situation. And then, a woman writing in Urdu in India or a man writing in Urdu in India would also be the same. Women have been writing in Urdu for the past hundred years. The first woman novelist wrote at more or less the same time as the first man novelist. The point - a woman writing self-consciously - and we return to a situation common to women all over the world.

S : But what of the cultural context? George Eliot had to adopt masculine *nom de plume* to escape the critical bias against women's writing in nineteenth-century England. Till about fifteen, twenty years ago the situation in India was perhaps the same? Did the evaluation of your work ever depend on your femininity, did that ever affect your self-consciousness for which you had to make an effort to rid yourself of while writing? In selecting the theme of your creative venture or the adoption of a stance?

QH: It may surprise many to know there has never been the kind of segregation of men and women in Urdu literature you might expect from a society that practices such segregation in life. I think we must understand this peculiar phenomenon at the outset. There have been women writing fiction and there have been women writing poetry. The male chauvinistic patronization –that one encounters anywhere in the world…I think it was never so emphatic here and the woman was not affected enough to be disturbed *as a writer*. She didn't have to worry. My own mother started writing at the age of thirteen or fourteen and there was no question of any criticism of the kind there would have been in the case of a woman coming out of *purdah* - a woman could have been writing even romantic short stories or novels.

As for me, what I am perturbed about is not this gender self- consciousness, but the fact that critics in Urdu are generally not attentive to what is happening in fiction at all. There is clear-cut neglect of fiction by the critic in general. There has been no serious critical focus on fiction in Urdu. My own writing suffers as a result.

S: Does that result in an exclusiveness of sorts or an isolation of the writer?

QH: No, I don't feel that at all. I am not an isolationist, nor am I a celebrator of loneliness. My concern is that my work suffers from the lack of any active and lively literary give and take - you know, a literary life, as it were. There is a general indifference. I don't mean that I *need* critics... nor do I need critics' certificates. Only, I feel bad about the neglect that fiction suffers from.

S: You think the creativity of the fiction writer is affected due to inadequate critical attention?

QH: Yes, indeed. The wrong kind of approach, coterie mentality and coterie politics which promote bad and mediocre literature can do a lot of harm. I have mentioned, a number of times, really outstanding fiction writers in my own writing and in interviews. Many people have not even heard of them, but there's never a follow-up. No-one asks me who they were, what they wrote, etc. In Urdu, there is a strong tendency to attach one's self to a single writer. For example a critic will start what he calls specializing on one writer, say, Premchand - he'll go on writing about him, his characters, bulls in his fiction, his village. 'Everything else in literature pales. His total devotion to Premchand blinds him to everything else. Another one may be devoted to Iqbal, and yet another perhaps to modern poetry. I think this amounts to taking an easy way out.

S: Is this a reflection of the complex diversity of our Indian society, wherein each great writer constitutes a category in himself? There is a diversification of concerns and the multiplicity of perspectives, the exposure to a variety of cultures and religions down the ages on the one hand, and on the other, the reception of technology and 'progress–oriented' modern civilization. In the west, movements and categories are used to classify writers – the literature of cruelty, of silence... while here, it becomes far more difficult to 'group' writers.

QH: But what I'd like to emphasize strongly is the *lack* of original thinking in critical writing here. It's so repetitive. The Progressive Movement began in 1936 and till today they are busy writing *reports* rather than criticism, producing surveys. This goes on year after year.

There is no criticism worth its name and the thinking is so

confused. For instance, the same writers who made such a laudatory hoo-ha about abstract and symbolistic writing ten years ago are now condemning it. It was supposedly a revolution in Urdu fiction and all earlier writing was rejected as backward and stupid. A lot of bad stories were recognized as *real* intellectual thinking, *real* inner life, etc. All those clichés were used for stories which were not even riddles – riddles can be much more interesting. The point is that there is no clear thinking and perhaps there is no clearly developed critical faculty.

S: Is there progress in writing itself? Your father Sajjad H. Yaldrum was himself an established short story writer in the realist style before the emergence of modernist techniques or perspectives. A generation later, you have been producing a very different kind of fiction, both long and short. Would you say that's 'progress' in literature and that you've taken the short story ahead? Or, is it just a question of how the writer confronts his own reality and gives his own kind of fictional representation to experience?

QH: I think there's definitely 'progress' in literature, which is after all influenced by the progress of the human mind. For instance, the philosophical probe into the concept of reality, or say the discovery of the theory of relativity; writers who were writing prior to this would have a different worldview. The general advancement of knowledge is bound to affect the sensibility of the writer. My father's generation was reading Tennyson and my generation was brought up, as it were, on T. S. Eliot and that itself makes all the difference. Of course, great literature will always be great irrespective of the age it's produced in. As Hazlitt says, the writer captures the 'spirit of his age'; it does not matter what technique he might use.

S: There are more and more tools available to comprehend the various dimensions of reality now, and the writer with her ingenuity finds newer modes of creative expression. I am reminded here of writers such as Samuel Beckett, and their frustration with the inadequacy of language vis-a-vis the expression of creative experience. And this is in English with its tremendous emphasis on the sociology and science of language. Despite that or perhaps because of the 'cacophony' produced by the 'explosion of words' and the 'language revolution', some writers are striving towards the 'literature of silence'. There is a lack of faith in the semantic potential of the 'word'. Do you take a similar position as a writer in Urdu, or has Urdu escaped this surfeit because it has not had similar attention paid to it?

QH: No, that is not my problem at all. Urdu is rich. There *is* a tremendous range of meanings around each word in Urdu. Yet I would not be able to cope with one single area of expression - a single dialect.

What concerns me, or rather disturbs me, is the gradual deterioration in the use of the language. I'm very bothered about the purity of language, wherein lies its beauty. I feel upset when I hear unwieldy Hindi being used on Doordarshan because Hindi is also a beautiful language. And they use ungainly expressions like *Mausam chipchipata rahega.* Well that's against the aesthetics of the language.

But as a writer in Urdu, I don't feel the inadequacy of language; I am simply aware that it has a lot to offer.

S: Your perceptive concern for history is striking, particularly in *Aag ka Darya.* You make large expanses of time and history available in the present in the novel. Do you feel constricted when you are writing a short story because the form does not allow one to spread out over the same length of time?

QH: Yes, but I think many of my stories do dwell over a long period of time. Some are about the whole life of a character, some about the life of a family. They tend to cover a number of phases in a lifetime, not just one little piece, or facet.

S: I find that your novels carry very poignant points of stasis that sometimes give your reader the feeling that you are far more comfortable writing a novel...What prompts you to choose the short story form? Is there any theoretical position that you take regarding the form you choose to write in?

QH: 1 think this whole business of theory... for me it doesn't mean anything. You write because you feel like writing... there's an idea you want to express.

S: But sometimes the writer makes a conscious effort to theorize the form she's choosing...

QH: May be they do...I have been interested in history and I have been using it in my fiction...

S: How do you respond to the idea of the annihilation of history, the modernist impulse to dissociate the "present" totally from the *sense* of history, to privilege instead an 'illusion of immediacy'?

QH: All these techniques and theories! They don't mean anything to me. What I feel interested in, I spontaneously write....

S: Well, if the technique is bound up with the theme, reflection on one aspect might yield clues,for the better comprehension of the other.

QH: I have been trying to explain to many people over and over again that technique comes *naturally* when one sits down to write. One does not have to consciously think about it. *It just happens.* With a musician, it is different. She has a *raag*. Though she may choose a variation, the constraints of the *raag* have to be adhered to. For me it is different. For me, mostly, some little scene, an image from my memory, starts me off. And then the technique evolves by itself. For instance, my recent novel *Gardishe Range Chaman*. I remember a scene... my mother was a pioneer of sorts in education and was very happy to meet educated women, particularly if a lady had gone "abroad" to study. Well, there was a lady who came to Lucknow as an inspector of schools. My mother and I went to see her. Hers was a house hidden in a garden with huge thick trees. There were two ladies there, two middle-aged, unmarried sisters, and the younger one, quite good looking, was the Inspector who'd been to England. Now, at that time this was quite a novelty. I'm talking of the 30's. On the mantelpiece inside the house there were some little ceramics. Strangely, we were told by the older woman that they were made by her when she'd joined an Arts School in England while she was chaperoning her younger sister in that country. Now, that scene remained in my mind. I never met them again... Here were two ladies, simple folks from a middle-class Muslim family...Who were they and what happened to them, I don't know. But that scene stayed with me. And much later over the years I started off with this novel with two ladies in a house in Lucknow. But they are mother and daughter. They've been to England; the younger one is a doctor and the mother says, "I did those paintings when my daughter was studying". You see, this is how for a writer anything like that is a starting point. I didn't sit down to work out the theme or the technique. I just started writing and the plot developed, the characters got going. I called it a semi-documentary novel because I brought in a lot of real people...

S: This is interesting –how a small image or a little happening develops into a huge novel. Actually, come to think of it, even a casual reader notices the use of the visual in your stories. It's cinematic, this concern for the *image* and also, the play that takes place in the handling of time, going back and forth and the use of the montage…

QH: It's cinematic...and I indulge in a little bit of painting too, so the concern for colours...

S: Your use of the stream of consciousness mingles with the narrative style. But you and other writers in this subcontinent have adapted this technique rather than using it in the manner of a Virginia Woolf. There's the linear sense of time, and there's then the dive *into* time.

QH: Perhaps...

S: I'd like to draw your attention to your contemporaries in Urdu. How do you respond to them? There's hardly any give and take between the writer and readers or critics, but what about your fellow-writers? Do you feel particularly curious about some and are you especially attracted or influenced or even disturbed by some? And do you discriminate between the writer from the west and the one writing in Urdu? There are some writers who seem to deliberately not read their own contemporaries.

QH: Oh, that'd be very sad. Not only do I read my contemporaries with interest, I have been translating some of them into English. It'd be carrying one's smugness a bit too far, to deliberately not read one's contemporaries.

S: There's also at times a total dependence or an imitative following of contemporaries. Or at times there's complete indifference or apathy; both are equally disturbing!

QH: It'd be silly to be like that. You are in fact enriched by looking around. There are four or five very significant writers in Urdu who've been actively writing as my contemporaries and I always read them.

S: How would you define modernism?

QH: It's very difficult because what you call modernism today-well, Shakespeare also may have called himself modern as compared to, say, Chaucer. Modernism is very relative. In the nineteenth century, say from Baudelaire onwards, they were all moderns. People writing in the earlier period, in the period of regency... well, Pope was modern in his times.

S: But if I'm referring specifically to the aesthetic, social, and scientific sense of the inadequacy of conventional forms in the early twentieth century...

QH: The conventional forms were shaken and broken even earlier, in France in the late nineteenth century. It came to us much later. But I wouldn't relate our situation with that because then we'd appear such Rip Van Winkles, or merely imitative. T.S. Eliot's *The Waste Land* was translated into Urdu around 1935 though it was written much earlier. Baudelaire was introduced in Urdu about a hundred years after his time as a 'modern' poet of France. The point is, when we use the term "modern" we automatically relate it to something that came to us from the west.

S: You don't think western 'modernism' entered the writer's consciousness even in the east, particularly in India where the British had entrenched English as a common language for communication?

QH: But you know even in our painting, Amrita Shergil who became our first modern was doing what had been done much earlier in Europe. So when we talk of modernism in India...

S: ... In the fifties...

QH: Oh, the fifties?! Well, don't ask me! What is it ...introspection, representation of inner life...

S: The same kind of concerns which one finds in English literature in the early twentieth century.

QH: Quite right - but then it's the delayed action one notices here. I am certainly not part of it. In fact I started all this - monologue, interior monologue, stream of consciousness, abstract thinking- in the forties when I was a teenager. So, I am a pioneer! Which is of course not acknowledged. My short stories in *Sitaron ke Aage* would bear me out. They demonstrate all those ideas which the second generation Urdu writers are trying to do. I did all that in my second year of graduation. All this is old hat for me. I've been through it long ago. And I did it unconsciously, not as a part of a movement.

S: Do you think something was added to what had already happened, in Europe? Or is our modernist literature a mere borrowing? Did you yourself feel that you were writing under the influence of such and such writer? Did say, the inner life of the Urdu writer in the forties and fifties determine her literary techniques? Or had the "new writer" not yet come into her own? Could we say the "modern" short story came into its own in Hindi and Urdu in the sixties and seventies, grappling with the gruesome aftermath of Partition, and it took that long because the *form* of the story is itself not indigenous?

QH: But Manto and Ahmed Ali had been producing great short stories since the thirties.

S: But in the fifties there's clear artificial insemination of ideas from abroad. The 'existential', the 'absurd', were being talked about amongst the intellectual elite and short stories were being woven over such philosophic base essentially western. So that the short-story appeared to be a sky-scraper precariously balanced without a foundation. A lot of experimental writing was being done. But it's only in late sixties that the 'modern' emerged as an evolved sensibility, isn't it? Writers such as Ram Lal, Bedi, and some others wrote in their identifiable voices.

QH: ... Ram Lal is a good writer in the narrative form. He makes for comfortable reading and is, what you may call a "natural" writer. Joginder Paul has been doing a lot of good philosophic and experimental writing.

S: Isn't the kind of magical realism one witnesses in the Latin American writers such as Garcia Marquez actually much closer to the way we perceive reality here than the perspectives yielded by the modernist writing from the west?

QH: Shall I confess to you, I have not been able to get

around to reading Marquez and the other South American writers one hears so much about these days...

S: It's just that I am struck by a sort of lack of critical acknowledgement regarding the presence of similarities between our perspectives and narratives and those of the Latin American culture.

QH: It's the rage these days. The business of writing consciously... I was in Sweden recently for a Seminar. A Professor read a bit from the Penguin reproduction of *Aag ka Darya* (I'm quite sick of this novel and try not to mention it). Well, what he said set me thinking about my total lack of interest in what I do. He read one chapter and said I wrote a 'total novel' much earlier than this American writer. And I didn't know what this 'total' novel is, and I of course didn't even know about Marquez. Well, that apart, I feel shocked that our critics are not examining fiction in the way a new piece of writing is taken up elsewhere in the world. Our fiction suffers from total neglect and the whole critical effort is concentrated on poetry.

S: Also, critical perspectives are being drawn from the west - structuralism, deconstruction, practical criticism, and so on. Surely, our literature could dictate its own critical canons and norms.

QH: Our critics seem to have nothing original to say. They go on *quoting*... this has been happening for the last forty years now. A long string of words and very little genuine analysis jumbled and obscure thinking!

S: Actually, there is a discernible, logical development of the modern short story in the subcontinent, a clear sense of the indigenous tradition that can be critically appreciated. Our native myths and archetypes have gradually got assimilated in this literary form and our traditional modes of writing, katha, dastaan, etc., have eventually got amalgamated with the new short story. I wonder why so few critics seem inclined to sort this out and establish the distinctive reality of the modern Indian short story. What happened rather abruptly in early twentieth century English literature slowly took root here with a difference and blossomed with different hues and shapes.

QH: I should think that the fundamental problem with our critics is that they don't read at all. What they read – some new critical books borrowed from the British Council or the U.S.I.S. – seems new and sensational and they start quoting left and right. Once they get important posts and chairs in the universities all they've to do is repeat themselves.

S: Would you say that the power to dictate critical standards is rather misplaced?

QH: The big names that begin to control the readership of literature here have done a lot of harm to the cause of good literature.

S: One more question - this business of inspiration which is at times over-romanticized, because writing definitely involves intense labour… Do you feel that you are taken over or possessed while you are in the process of writing. What is your state of mind?

QH: Oh, no, not at all. I don't go by that sort of thing. I have no belief in the occult or the spiritual.

S: And whatever you produce, does that become itself only in the process of writing or is it a well-planned venture?

QH: No, I don't sit down and plan an entire plot. It's a kind of a rough plan at the outset which gets developed as I write.

S: That was a truly free and open discussion on some of the fundamental problems regarding the creative process and critical assessment of modern fiction in Urdu. Thanks indeed for your uninhibited expression!

Nirmal Verma

On the Modern Short Story in Hindi

NIRMAL VERMA

Padma Bhushan, Sahitya Akademi Fellow, Jnanpith awardee and Chevalier de l'ordre des arts et des lettres NIRMAL VERMA *(1929-2005) took his Master's degree in History from St. Stephen's College, Delhi. In 1959, on the invitation of the Czechoslovak Oriental Institute, Verma went to Prague for a decade, to translate modern Czech authors into Hindi. In short order he published not only translations of three Czech novels, two collections of short stories, and a play, but also his own first novel* Ve Din *(Those Days) in 1964, a collection of short stories called* Jalti Jhari *(The Burning Bush) in 1965, and several volumes of travelogues and reminiscences. After his return to India he served as Fellow at the Indian Institute of Advanced Study in Shimla to explore mythic consciousness in literature. He was invited to the Iowa International Writing Programme in 1977.*

Verma has been as prolific as he was influential. Sixteen collections of short stories, nine novels, eleven collections of essays, three autobiographical works, and a play by him are currently in print and housed in the American Library of Congress as significant world literature. His work has been translated and published by Oxford University Press, Penguin, Readers International, Indialog, and Orient Blackswan, among others; his oeuvre is critical material for any university-level appreciation of Hindi literature.

He was also a career activist: starting with Gandhi's prayer meetings through 1947-48 and via membership of the Communist Party of India till 1956 – when he resigned following the Soviet Union's invasion of Hungary. His work is formally modernist – twentieth-century loneliness is his central theme, and his preoccupation with form is legendary. Verma is credited with pioneering the 'nayi kahani' (new story) in Hindi. But the delicacy of touch with which he examines the vulnerabilities of the human condition is more closely aligned with the work of continental and British writers of the nineteenth century too...

SUKRITA: Going through the gamut of short stories written in Hindi over the past several decades, one cannot help concluding that a lot of them have been written with a different orientation from earlier fiction in Hindi, perhaps through the influence of the modernist wave arriving from the west. But literary criticism does not seem to be directed at sorting out any of the basic critical questions that arise from an orientation that involves an interaction between two cultures. To what extent is the writer able to locate her own native cultural identity? And how does she imbibe the influences from the west – is that at the cost of her own Indian psyche? And lastly, would you agree that a much more conscious and concerted critical effort is required for the evaluation of modern literature in Hindi?

NIRMAL VERMA: I totally agree that there hasn't been any focussed critical attention given to this issue. The authentic, indigenous contribution of a short story writer and what kind of exposure the writer has had to western writing, unconsciously and at times rather indiscriminately, are important features that have not been formulated or identified clearly by critics in Hindi. I think the reason is that for a long time 'influences' have been regarded very suspiciously, and somehow much criticism of contemporary Indian writing is aimed at proving that even the best of it is derivative. Whether our writing has indeed become a mere exercise in imitation or, as you've just said, there is a very creative sort of a confluence of the native and western sensibility in evidence, has not been worked out. This has obviously led to the impoverishment of the Indian critical scene. Perhaps I ought not to broadly say 'Indian' but then, as my friends from Karnataka, Bengal, or Maharashtra say the situation is not very different in Kannada, Bengali, or Marathi. What I do wonder, though, why you should feel it necessary to talk to the writers at all; you can always go to their works which I'd say are more eloquent than the writers themselves who may in fact mislead you.

S: Because I think it's important to see what some of the perceptive critics and writers consciously think about the questions I'm raising. Since there isn't a specific tradition that might give one perspective on the evaluation of modern Hindi literature, the teamwork involved with these interviews, the dialogue about styles and subjects, helps me be more objective and to determine how conscious or self-conscious writers of the subcontinent are, about western borrowings.

For you -- the characters of your short stories are not specifically related to a nation or a culture; they could be living anywhere in the world and do not seem to call for any situational localization. They could belong to any country. And the relationships, whether in *Parinde* or *Andhere mein*, are displaced relationships with a kind of quaintness about them. There is very little dialogue to reveal their psyche. However, you create an atmosphere in each story that matches the psychic uprootedness of the characters. In *Parinde* it is the mountains that give the story its atmosphere, not Shimla the city. Is modernity responsible for the deeper connections characters seem to have with the elements – with the mountains – than with each other? Does the story acquire a more universal character, somehow, through this kind of representation?

NV: This is a very interesting point. Writers are sometimes not aware of what pattern or quality of life emerges from their work. I'd say many of my stories are a reflection of the Indian middle-class milieu, and some of the silences are an integral part of the inarticulate suffering of middle-class individuals in our society. So much of the inner anguish articulated in western, word-oriented societies becomes inevitably muffled and convoluted through indirectness in the Indian context. For example, if a girl is in love with a person she is not able to make this feeling coherent, either to her own self or to another person.

Second, the point you have made regarding the elements. I'd rather put it this way - I feel deeply fascinated by the invisible relationship between the action of the story and its ambiance, where it is taking place, and the process through which a larger relationship is established, not merely amongst the individuals in the story but between the individuals and something non-human. The mountains in *Parinde*, a certain climate, a certain time of the year, say the autumn - these are things to which I always like to relate myself as well as my characters, maybe to feel emotionally secure as to the particular situation of the story's dramatic trajectory. So, as far as I'm able to formulate it coherently, a sort of unspecific, invisible but very sensuous and tangible environment in which the characters are operating - whether it is the mountains or the cityscape or season – is imperative. Specific localities aren't important, but their particularities and peculiarities are. This is what particularizes the situation, and that seems to give a story its universal dimension.

S: The story, then, is not confined within political boundaries, nor are any geographical limits established.

NV: Let me just add one thing - sometimes I feel very fascinated by it - this feeling of being cramped within individual relationships has another counterpoint in some of my stories, where this extra-human dimension, this non-human provides an experience of tremendous relief to the characters. They feel that even though there may not be a way out of the tangled tender relationships, there is something much bigger than them - the infinity of the skies, the continuity - the eternal continuity - of certain things around them. Those things stand as a counterpoint to something that is happening in a very immediate human context.

S: Yes! I did note, as a reader, that the relatedness between characters and elements seems to bring about a kind of harmony to the situation and the tension in human relationships seems to get resolved, lending a sense of relief and a psychological equilibrium.

NV: Also, I'd say, it gives perspective.

S: Which brings me to the impact of the short story on the reader. Let us speak of Indian readers in particular - obviously at some level you are conscious of the kind of readership you have. There appears to be a wide gap between the writer's and the Indian reader's measure of understanding and awareness. The writer is of course often ahead of her time. Even so, she does desire, not recognition, but some immediate response from the reader. What is your experience as a writer in India where a large percentage of people are not able to respond to what is called 'modern literature'? The consensus seems to be that modern literature is sometimes perhaps *abusively* modern. How do you respond to this attitude? And how does it affect your writing?

NV: It is easy to answer this question because in India we who claim to be educated get accustomed to living or working in a self-created insularity. This can be very frustrating for a writer who is trying to get readers to see or feel past their insularity. The problem is greater than the writer not being able to get a response. It is a sociological problem. One is so conditioned to insularity after a while one stops feeling bothered by it and thinking about whether this is healthy or unhealthy. I do think that this has vast, disturbing implications but I shall not go into them now. However, I'd like to emphasize another point - that my literature or anything that gives meaning to one's existence, or whatever matters to one - you can't share those things with many people, so you get intuitively attached to the coterie of those with whom you can. People - friends, fellow-writers or readers - who are responding to you. This can work out to be negative. You feel so frustrated by the critics that you stop taking notice of them because you feel that their criticism or appreciation is so off the mark you don't feel flattered or happy even if they say anything good, nor do you feel dejected if criticized. But that means you stop listening to anyone outside a small group – and that too is insularity.

S: I'd say that young writers in India need extraordinary perseverance to sustain their efforts in light of the discomfiture of an unsympathetic critical atmosphere. We may in fact be losing a lot of genuine writers in the process.

NV: Sure, sometimes that is what causes a rather late maturity or an early death for writers. This is a sociological problem again. The creative exchange between an alert readership and the writer or between critics and the writer can make a world of difference.

S: Another question. In the west 'modernism' is not only a specific literary stirring but also the consequence of a cultural crisis which comes with fragmentation within the psyche, diffusion of values, the rise of a hyper-questioning mind and a breakdown of the assurance of faith. Witness the Nietzschean declaration that "God is dead". As a result of all this there was "a lost generation", the Bloomsbury group, and tremendous number of experiments in literary form. All of these fit into a sort of a pattern. In India, however, one does see the impact of modernism, but the roots lie elsewhere? Do you think the Indian psyche has gone through a similar crisis, which might explain the acceptance of some of western modernism's literary features assimilated into Indian literatures?

NV: I should think that the traumas of Europe through this century are very different in nature from the type of disruptions and discontinuities that have gripped Indian society in our times.

S: There is a similarity of sensibilities in modernist writing from the two diverse cultures - for instance a Kafka short story sometimes aligns totally with a short story in Hindi or Urdu. So, despite the difference in cultural contexts, there seems a similarity in thematic concerns.

NV: I am not so sure about that. Do Hindi and Urdu writers have the same sense of cataclysmic horror or metaphysical vacuity or the same quest for something which could give meaning to one's existence that writers such as Beckett, Kafka, and Camus do? ...I wonder if there really are any parallels or Indian counterparts.

S: Well, take loneliness and alienation in JeelaniBano's short story *Main,* Ramlal's story *Bheed* or Joginder Paul's *Bhabho.* These stories pointedly deal with the suffering of the individuals from feeling 'unrelated' to their environs, feeling uprooted, and there is that striving to locate their identities. There seems to be a rather grotesque oscillation between complete loss of self and hypersensitivity to the self.

NV: I have not read these stories and am in no position to authentically or legitimately comment on them. There are, however, many types of alienation and there are many qualities of loneliness ... the loneliness or the solitariness of a sanyasi living on the mountains is very different from the loneliness of an individual in Paris, or even the loneliness of an individual in India living in a big city like Bombay is very different in texture from the very individuated feeling of anguish and loneliness of a person living in New York. So, a very specific type of comparison has to be made, between two individuals in stories written in two entirely different milieus, otherwise talking about loneliness is too abstract. I think for a critic it should be fascinating to make specific distinctions between, say, loneliness in a 'tradition-ridden' society like India where families are nevertheless breaking up, and the loneliness in a 'liberated' western society.

S: And while these differences stare hard at the reader she may identify with the alien in such a complete way that the 'universal' emerges easily... I mean when an Indian reads Beckett's *Waiting for Godot,* with all its specific contexts, the way the characters are trying to define Godot for themselves, he may see his own desire to identify with the ubiquitous Self in this pattern. And yet many an Indian rejects Beckett, if only in denial of such identification.

NV: You know, only a very deeply religious person could write such an anguished play. Unless there is a deep crisis of faith within us, that God did exist and now I have lost him, unless this having of it earlier and then the experience of having lost it is there we wouldn't even have the capacity to receive the experience represented in the play. We would just take the external wrappings of a Beckett without any real understanding of the inner core of the crisis out of which his meaning acquired urgency. Now, how many writers in India have passed through this dark night of the soul and emerged like this ... I agree that at one time I had a beautiful relationship with the almighty ... or maybe my forefathers had a beautiful intimate relationship with something that also sustained me, but since religious faith itself has become a matter of irrelevance, there is no question of the agony of the loss. There is simply nothing, and the sense that something *was*. The point I'm trying to make is that during the last fifty or sixty years a kind of pseudo-secularized culture has developed in our cities. Neither are we religious nor so individuated that we write an entirely different set of values from that of the religious past; we are enmeshed between here and there. The horror of the death of God is only real for a person who really wanted a world sustained by some power. Similarly, *Samskara* by Ananthamurthy - who in an indirect manner describes this feeling in a brahmin - alienated from his traditional bondage and spiritual torment.... I personally feel that Ananthamurthy does not succeed in his aim because he superimposes a western existential dilemma on the psyche of the brahmin - but the story could be a very genuine, rich dilemma for a fictional character. Yet the reading and the writing of it depends on the sort of faith one has.... I can appreciate Beckett but I cannot recreate dilemmas such as his; they do not emanate from my own climate. If they are part of my own feeling that yes, there are certain values that are disintegrating and that I love those values and that I feel the loss of those values, then I might.

And as a reader, there are so many associations that you find in *Waiting for Godot*... so many spiritual and religious symbols you find in Kafka; without a close understanding of their contexts one has to read these texts very, very closely to discern all the fine complexities.

S: Would you agree that if one can creatively identify oneself as a reader with a certain experience that comes from the west, one does succeed in living it; and, if one is living it the vicarious 'experience' would create a similar sensibility, which in turn would produce similar artefacts?

NV: It would depend on whether this 'experience' triggers something in me that deeply involves me - otherwise I may just be a passive admirer of a western writer without his having any direct influence on what I'm trying to pursue or write.

S: But you do think an experience can by itself cause a modification of the sensibility?

NV: It would depend a lot on what I am looking for in my own writing and my reading may give an additional dimension to my original pursuit. Naturally then it'll become a creative part of my spiritual equipment; otherwise it may be merely an encumbrance.

S: It is sometimes argued that the Indian cultural orientation does not allow an easy acceptance of 'change'. The concern for the 'new' is resisted by readers, and many a time even the psyche of the writer resists the idea of experimentation and innovation. In the west there is a call for progress, innovation, and change with a great sense of urgency. How do you look at this? Do you think people in India cling too much to the past and does that cause stagnation? Do you see this tendency in Hindi?

NV: We are an uprooted generation. And we did not even pass through a meaningful assessment of the rich relevance of our myths.

S: Yes, there has not been much creative use of the past.

NV: In about ninety nine percent of Indian writing there is in fact not even a mechanical use of the past. We are living, it seems, without any mythological past. The present seems to have nothing to do with that rich heritage. This, I think, is a great deprivation.

S: Coomaraswamy talks perceptively of the creative continuation of tradition. Perhaps it's one of the ills of colonial conditioning: it's either an absolute rejection of the past or a rigid adherence to the beliefs and attitudes of old times while the world has marched so far ahead.

NV: But I miss even the genuine conservatives. There are none now. It is a pleasure to see a real brahminical zealot! But there aren't even any superficially sincere conservatives around.

S: I think the current critical milieu neither encourages nor takes stock of truly modernist creative ventures – if they did I think it would help tremendously, perhaps cause a resurgence of new ideas and a regeneration of old myths.

NV: To cause a further sense of disillusionment and add to the cynicism of the situation ... let me tell you, this is not limited to academia. Even in the writing community, while there is much conversation on social change, revolutions, varieties of Marxism etc. most writers do not have even an elementary understanding of the relationship between the world of Indians today and the types of social structures that were created in our epics. This ought to be the closest thing to me as a contemporary writer. I feel that very few of us even feel the *loss* of that connection which a western writer so automatically has with his past, though *his* past is apparently more dead than mine ... We as a society are much more involved in our old rituals and traditions...

S: western writers such as Yeats and Eliot who turned to the east...

NV: That is precisely the result ... India seems to have more to offer to the west than to its own selves...

S: Through the twentieth century political movements in the west went along with philosophic theories on and scientific analyses of new sociological phenomena. Writers such as Huxley, Sartre, and Grass have a sharp political consciousness that merges with their artistic consciousness. On the other hand, in Indian literature the political commitment of the writer, rather than enriching the artistic version, has often corrupted literary ventures. One witnesses a lot of propaganda in the name of political concern in Indian literature, doesn't one?

NV: You are absolutely right. The reason lies in what we were discussing earlier. We have lost the traditional enclaves of our own cultural frontiers and because of that loss we easily become servile to any political tendency from outside. We make no effort to absorb the political current within our own cultural milieu, as happens in the west. In the west there is an entire tradition of discourse, philosophical discourse in the universities, periodicals, and magazines. All political movements get filtered through, even structuralists and linguists become *aware* of them rather than servile to them. They then try to understand the relevance and meaning of those movements vis-a-vis their own discipline.

S: In that case rejection is as meaningful as absorption.

NV: Since we have built no structures for the appropriate filtration of new ideas in the name and fashion of modernism, not only have we lost the traditional structures, we have made no headway evolving new ones which may be in consonance with life today. We are stuck between 'right' and 'left' dogmas. We have, in other words, become servile and servility, I'm afraid, can never result in creativity.

S: How would you reconcile the idea of 'progress' with the early twentieth century movement towards 'primitivism' spearheaded by D.H. Lawrence in literature? Is there any progress in literature which implies that the twentieth century literary artefact is more refined or better than before?

NV: I sometimes wonder whether this concept of 'progress' is not a mere illusion, not merely in literature but in every sphere of our lives. In one respect I think as Eliot said we can see more than our ancestors - if you insist on calling it 'progress' you may say it is 'more'... But even if you do, you also have to acknowledge that something *more* is *there* because we dwarfs are sitting on the shoulders of all time, of giants through time. A dwarf can see more, precisely because he is sitting on the shoulders of time, but he does not become bigger than that giant, or more far-seeing. So when I read a 'past' classic there is never an obstacle within me preventing me from enjoying it or getting real sustenance from it merely because it was written in the sixteenth or seventeenth century. It is as perfect a work of art as a work of art composed in my own time can be.

S: Shakespeare is as contemporary to us as to his own age...

NV: So, this entire sociological concept of linear 'progress' is now being discarded even in its own disciplines, in history and sociology. If we adopt it in literature, there will be a crisis. And yet if I have to say how one work of art responds, not merely to the situation outside but also to the preceding work of art, there is a certain continuous relationship not only between art and society but also between one work of art and another work of art.

S: And it is this continuity that lends the work its quality of endurance.

NV: Yes, and therefore I cannot imagine for instance, Proust without his own predecessors and I cannot imagine that many of the writers today have not imbibed quite as much, even though it may not be very visible because most creative influences are really so pervasive that you are not able to identify whether it is something joyous or…

S: The essentials remain the same and yet there have been changes. In the linear time, even if *man* has lost his tail ... he has remained a man all the same.

NV: That can be the only answer.

S: Another question: there seems to be a self- conscious delineation of Indian *culture* and a presentation of its distinctiveness to the outside world. Some literary writing in India is being done from the point of view of its appeal to the 'foreigner'. Don't you think there is an urgent need on the part of the Indian writer to liberate herself from, shall I say, exhibitionism of a kind?

NV: Yes, indeed. But I don't think very much of that kind of writing will survive and we have to carefully sift the 'genuine' from the 'phony'.

S: Would you agree that today a whole lot of writing is passing for literature which should merely have received cursory attention? What would you have to say about literary awards at the national level today?

NV: I had a very bad experience at Frankfurt where I found that German writers are not as concerned about the quality of contemporary writing in India as they are in knowing which particular part in India, which region or community the writer comes from. If somebody is writing about tribals, she becomes more important. If somebody is writing from the point of view of a 'Harijan' they get interested. For them what is significant is representation of say, an ethnic minority. This is a very disturbing phenomenon. I made this point in one of the meetings in Bhopal once - that about a hundred years ago tourists from abroad came to see our magicians, road-dancers and our snake charmers. Now they come to see our representatives from various exotic minorities and whether we are writing about tribal communities or characters or about the scheduled castes this seems to me 'extra'-literary criteria applied to our writing.

S: There is then a rather patronizing and condescending attitude. Perhaps the product is 'consumer oriented' for its marketability. The demand is catered to and the approach becomes more and more commercial. Even political patronage may be accorded to such writing.

NV: As in the Soviet Union, for example, writers with definite communist leanings were translated with greater alacrity than those who were different.

S: As to the form of the short story... I think it was Chekov who said that once a short story has been written the beginning and the end should be deleted and the middle that remains constitutes the short story. In India the tradition of katha is the indigenous Indian form of the short story. But what we have in the modern Indian short story does resemble the western mode of short fiction. Obviously then, there has been same transference of western ideas in Indian literature too, along with the transfer of the form of the short story. Has any critical theorization rationalized the formulation of such a feature?

NV: Very little, I'm afraid. Actually, this debate has become important very recently - whether the novel or short story genres which developed in peculiar historical circumstances in Europe ... should they not perhaps have a different structure and form in the Indian context which has an entirely different tradition of narratives. You are absolutely right that the discussion of the specific indigenous form of the narratives which ought to take place has not acquired any coherent theory as such. Though I must say that Hazari Prasad Dwivedi wrote some of his novels very much in the Puranic scheme in which one thing comes out of another and the linear development is not disrupted. This has given food for thought to the critic. But of course, there is still no proper discourse or reflection...

S: One finds a fairly free use of Joycean 'stasis' in the Indian short story, but it's not merely a borrowed technique. Again, while it is owned by writers, critics seem to hardly take notice of it. Have writers themselves reflected on this?

NV: Very little. Years ago, I wrote an article on the form of the Indian novel. That created quite a controversy. I also commented on and questioned Premchand's use of the realist form. It was never picked up in literary critical discourse ...

S: Who in Hindi, do you think, from amongst your contemporaries, projects the literary sensibility we have been discussing?

NV: I think the first name that comes to my mind is that

of Phanishwar Renu. In a very unconscious manner he tried to bring certain very interesting experiments into the novel.

S: Yes, I am familiar with his representation of the contemporary Indian peasant...

NV: So, one can be 'modern' without being affected by western sensibility. And Dwivedi and Renu are unique examples of 'indigenous modernity' which has nothing to do with western sensibility.

S: Since Renu is himself very much part of the rural set up of his stories, his concerns smack of no 'romantic' yearning for the pastoral. It is a very authentic confrontation with the real.

NV: On the other hand, Hazari Prasad Dwivedi remains a very urban intellectual pundit, very much concerned with the traditional forms of Indian religions. Renu and he derived their inspiration from different directions - one from the pastoral and the other from the urban socio-traditional. Dwivedi used to say that I have written my novels in *Gup Shaili* (gossip) which is very much a native style…

S: Talking about such a literary style will take us into post-modernism which should perhaps become the topic for our next sitting. Thank you very much for your direct and candid responses.

Jeelani Bano

On the Creative and the Critical

JEELANI BANO

Padma Shri JEELANI BANO has served as chairperson or principal advisor for a variety of non-governmental organizations that address systemic inequalities based on gender and the vulnerability of young people. She has also been on the Urdu advisory panel of the Sahitya Akademi as well as the National Book Trust. Her five novels, eleven short story collections, several books of poetry and screenplay of a film directed by Shyam Benegal have won her multiple awards, including the Maharashtra Urdu Academy Award, the Qaumi Hali award from the Haryana Urdu Academy, as well as literary awards in Pakistan and Qatar. Bano's professional intent has always been revolutionary: born to an orthodox family, she was also influenced by the Progressive Writers frequenting her poetically inclined parental home; her own inclination has pursued social justice and the preservation of Urdu – especially the Telegu-inflected Dakhini Urdu. Bano's books have been translated into a number of Indian languages, English, German, Norwegian, and Russian; she is herself a translator of Malayali short fiction. She has travelled to Tajikistan, Pakistan, Russia, and Uzbekistan for literary events, and is acknowledged as a stalwart of contemporary Urdu writing in the subcontinent.

SUKRITA: I found your story "Main" ("I" in English) fascinating – the loss of identity experienced by the protagonist and expressed so pointedly coheres with my definition of the modernist sensibility. And that specific experience acquires universal significance and meaning. It appears to be the story of each one of us existing in the contemporary milieu. Though the cause and explanation for this feeling may differ, we seem to end up with a similar consciousness on one level or another. Your other writing does not project this aspect of modern life significantly, but in "Main" you've presented a displaced character very convincingly. What is the source of this concern? Did you pick up on this theme from your general observation of modern life or is it related with any actual personal experience? Would you like to talk about the inspiration for this story, which is so different from your usual thematic concerns?

JEELANI BANO: It is very difficult for a writer to say where she or he may have found a certain story. It's possible that out of thousands of stories floating around, one particular story decides to come to me, on its own. And then I may own it, but to be able to say from where I acquired it becomes a puzzle for me too. Sometimes one may not pick up a whole story but just a part of it, maybe just one snippet from an actual event. I think I can relate "Main" with something that happened years ago. I remember a visiting relative who casually made a comment to my mother – about a one-and-a-half year old infant playing in front of them. She said the child couldn't be hers since he did not resemble her at all. I was touched by the reaction of the child – who howled and protested and wanted those words taken back. The incident triggered a chain of ideas in my mind. I said to myself, "Suppose a mother disclaims her child, what's likely to happen to the psyche of the child?" It might create a crisis of identity, with which he'd have to live all his life. At times mothers may make such statements in anger, and create a permanent feeling of insecurity in a person. There are occasions when one has a strange feeling of not belonging to the people around one or to the place one has apparently lived all one's life. What can one attribute this experience to? Everything gets to be so negative and unreal and all one is actually trying is to locate, to connect with one's self. Throughout one's life.

S: The beauty of that story is that a very broad abstract concept has acquired a specific shape and context. 'Modern' does not mean people in the past did not experience reality in this way. But a certain crisis of culture, the scepticism and cynicism following the First World War, did give rise to some fundamental philosophical questions regarding human existence. When I examined Urdu fiction, I noticed this phenomenon presented in the late 50's and 60's. The modernist sensibility projects itself in the 'new story' then. But somehow one doesn't witness the writer's exploration or search for new forms of expression. Perhaps retaining the old forms is a symptom of a conservative desire to remain with tradition. Have you ever felt the need to break the conventional form?

JB: I have no problem with the existing forms. As you said, in Europe there was a lot of philosophical cultural activity in the early twentieth century. We've been influenced by western thought too. But I would not say that there was any dearth of experimentation in Urdu. And, I don't think that the changes in our literature were entirely due to what happened in the west. We have always had our own philosophical base and we have had our own style of literary expression. I often resist the idea of reading, for instance, particularly when I'm in the process of writing fiction myself. It disturbs my frame of mind; the world of the book I may be reading interferes with the world I am in the process of creating. I regard it very important to retain the authenticity of the universe, the characters that I am creating. I hate to have any external shadow cast on them. I'd think no writer likes the idea of having anything superimposed on her or his own creation. If the work is to be original and not imitative, she'd better be able to safeguard her own world of her own fiction. I have been engaged in a lot of experimentation, too. I don't believe one has to necessarily conform to the existent patterns of short stories. I think any new story comes with its own style. We do not pre-plan its structure or style. The style is dependent on the nature of the content. The story told is not an event reported by the writer. It acquires the identity of a short story only when it is contained in its style, traditional or modern. My story "Ashtray main sulgatahua cigarette" ("A cigarette burning in the ashtray") is the story of an ordinary woman burning perpetually like a cigarette, with no one to listen to her, not even her husband. She's not a person to him but a domestic entity to look after his home and fulfill his physical desires. Her husband is a heavy cigarette-smoker and she's shown in the story to liken her existence with that of the cigarettes being smoked and discarded by the male at will...

S: The experience of womanhood is central to the next question I want to pose to you. As a woman writer of Urdu in a rather conservative society, what kind of problems do you face? What kind of self-consciousness has been created in you because you are a woman? Do you feel alienated in the men's world of writing and publishing? Are you conscious of having avoided certain themes because you are a woman? What kind of constraints have you laboured under as a woman writer? What are the encroachments on your freedom?

JB: I have never curbed myself, or not written on a particular theme because I am a woman. Nor have I ever thought of my gender as a limitation. I've always felt free to give expression to whatever I have been gripped by. How society may respond has not bothered me. But when I started writing I did face discomfiture. I belonged to a very conservative family from a feudal society of Badayuni, especially on my maternal side. My father was a scholar, a poet in Arabic and Persian, and was liberal enough to want his daughters to feel free. But my mother was very orthodox and she imposed a lot of restrictions on our movements. She followed purdah and one could not go unescorted anywhere, nor could one face a male visitor without purdah.

I started to write when I was about ten years old. Since my father was a poet, there used to be lots of poets visiting us. I remember how I used to wonder for long hours about how one could create anything original. I used to look at the poets with great reverence - Josh, Jigar, Sagar Nizami, Shakeel Badayuni, Qatil Shifai. I used to think of them as unusual beings who may have come from strange distant lands. When I started writing seriously and sending my work for publication, there was a lot of resistance from my mother. She thought no one would marry me as I was beginning to correspond with men in the publishing world. Indeed, I owe a lot to my father who let me go on. And then I got married at a rather early age, that is, immediately after my Intermediate. My father was keen to marry me to a person with literary taste, who'd not object to my writing. I had already published a book when I got married to Anwar who chose to marry me primarily because of my involvement in writing. I have been writing for the past 26-27 years and he has been very cooperative and understanding. I have been writing consistently throughout. I have no hurdles on the domestic front.

As for the social aspect or the literary world, I do have a complaint… about being neglected by the Urdu literary world. When I was young I used to hear, "Oh, in spite of being a woman, she writes well!" This is objectionable - the way one is put into a separate category of 'women writers'. As it is in big social get-togethers in our society, in literature too a separate enclosure seems to have been created for women. Temperamentally I do not anyway like to socialize too much with other people - writers in particular. I notice that in their so called literary meets, there's talk about everything but literature. I don't fit in such meetings. And perhaps that's why my name doesn't figure when they pass names around for awards etc. There's a lot of politicking involved in that. I remain out of it.

S: Regarding the 'award culture' that occupies a large space in our society today, what do you think, does that help build standards of literary production? Excellent work is being produced in Hindi and Urdu. Would you say that awards are given fairly, without biases of any kind?

JB: Our critics suffer from 'groupism'. Each established critic seems to have built up her or his own coterie of writers. They patronize only those of their own group. I have never played to their egos, nor have I ever joined any group. Why would they pay attention to me then? I figure in no books. Our literary scene is full of politics. The writers are like bonded labour. God knows why they go on writing! I ask myself why I keep writing all day. I am not going to receive either material gain or appreciation. Then there's the category of evaluators, who are going to make a business out of the writer's production and labour. I am busy writing in my frenzy but someone else is going to measure its worth and cash in on it. He might raise the work to the heavens in praise or condemn it to hell. He's the one to create its market value, tears it to pieces or gets it an award. You are no longer a part of your work. The writer, in our society, is totally bypassed. You must have noticed that in literary functions the writer generally occupies a back seat. The honoured guest will either be a minister or some chairperson of some academy. In such functions prescriptive speeches are made: "The writer should write for her race, for her nation". Ironically - given how uncertain writers themselves are of their function - the speaker always feels authorized to play the role of a guide to the writer. The writer appears a non-entity.

S: Elsewhere, the writer seems to be much more concerned with the political and the social scene. Here the reader and the writer don't seem to be in communication. The writer seems to be functioning rather isolatedly. Even established writers do not easily step in actively on social, moral, or political issues.

JB: I think the writer is not given a chance to do so.

S: May be writers need to reach their readers directly, without dependence on the "middlemen", the critics who have their own vested interests in promoting or demolishing a writer. The standards that ought to be maintained in literature can be totally dismissed in the political mire. The writer must build a direct rapport with her audience…

JB: But as writers we have neither sources nor resources. The writer has no control even over media. Tell me, do you see any worthwhile literary programmes on television? If there's a programme it's managed by non-writers and the popular item is 'humorous mushairas'. Morning T.V. programmes have a feature on some societal personality. Have you ever seen a literary figure, a Marathi, Hindi, or Telugu writer? Actually classical musicians are given much more time on T.V. or radio than writers. The fee offered to a musician is much higher, too. A writer is given no importance.

S: But then the increase in the number of literary awards also means that literary activity is being given importance. But I'd say what's required is a genuine critical examination of literary works, awards do nothing to build a critical tradition. If the awards are given in with a partisan outlook, indiscriminately, this does more harm than good to the cause of literature. Time remains the finest test for excellence in literature. But awards do play a role in drawing attention to a work of art.

JB: As far as I am concerned, awards have no value and I do not write for any appreciation at all. There was hardly any literary award in this country when I began writing.

S: Do you think that feminist criticism replaces one bias with another or would you say that there is a need for re-consideration of female perspectives in a literary work?

JB: Of course there's a need for this reaction. I don't think we have anybody working in that direction in contemporary Urdu literature. I wish we had. I do feel there's a need to examine female writing differently. I don't go by the belief that men and women receive experience in the same way. There is a difference and we have to give each its place. There's a distinct female perspective in literature and art. It'd certainly be wrong not to acknowledge that fact or to dismiss it.

S: How would you define 'modernism'? And how do you compare post-independence Urdu fiction with pre-independence?

JB: When claims of being 'new' or 'modern' are made for the latter fiction, I'd like to pause and consider how any literary work can be absolutely new or modern. It can change the old a little but it cannot be totally new. Styles of storytelling do change along with time. In Urdu, one does see evidence of changes in style and content in the short story. But I can't go along with the claim that in the 60's the story changed into something absolutely new. If anyone tried to make a total break with the tradition of the story, she ceased to produce a story. The narrative did not have the elements that make a story, nor did it reach its readers. But any short-story written at any time, if it is good, is a new story: it has not been written earlier and that is why it's fresh. If it had existed earlier it need not have been re-written. Our society has been changing. We do not have the same kind of problems today that we had, say, ten years ago. Our feelings, our thoughts are changing and the world is getting smaller. The content of our short stories too is thereby changing. The stream of time keeps flowing and changing directions and our sensibility goes along with it; so does its expression in art. I don't think any one period stands out distinctly as 'modern' or entirely different.

S: Would you say that there's any 'progress' in literature? With more specialized disciplines in 'knowledge' available to us, have we got a firmer grip over our existence and if so, is it reflected in art?

JB: No, I don't think there's any such thing as 'progress' in literature. The '60s short story in Urdu acquired a rather peculiar feature in the name of 'modernity': the story lost its 'story-ness', recoiled into a strange insular world that people could not understand. It's a different matter if I write a story and keep it with myself but if I write and ask others to read it - well, some kind of communication has to be established. The story is between you, the reader, and me, the writer. Reading it does not necessarily mean that you like it. But if part of it has remained with you, then the story has meaning for me as well. If you do not retain any part of it and return the entire story to me, then that story is meaningless for me as well. If the story does not have the capacity to reach anyone then it is not worth its existence. It's important for a story to have the element of 'story-ness'. Its narration should attract attention and it should be absorbing.

S: When you read other writers, have you ever felt that you wished you could write like anyone of them? Have there been any writers whose influence you may have wanted to shake off?

JB: Camus used to impress me tremendously. And I read Gorky when I was quite young. I felt very moved by *The*

Mother. Chekov, too, impressed me a lot but I have never felt I should write like anyone of them or be like them. You know, sometimes I get so deeply involved in my stories it's almost as though I get entangled in a snare. Even in the night, I'm haunted, and when I get down to my domestic chores in the morning, the world of my writing casts a heavy shadow on everything and I desire absolute isolation. When I was writing my story "Cultural Academy" I met the character called Usha in a dream at a get-together in which somebody introduces her to me. She did not respond to me. In the morning – believe me, it was a strange experience dealing with her in my writing, having seen that character in the dream.

S: At times perhaps the world of fiction is more real than the world in which one actually has to operate in.

JB: When I am involved in a story, I am very mechanical in my 'actual" world. When I am totally submerged and ridden with tension I go to the kitchen and do things that have nothing to do with the story.

About this matter of what is 'real' – my writing itself has to tell me how real it is. I don't go by any other voices. When I was writing my recent novel on bonded labour I had thought of delineating Salim in one way, but after I had written a part of the book I realized it had.acquired a different colour. The character wanted to be different from how I had conceived him. I generally give in when such a clash occurs.

S: Thank you so much for making the reality of your fictional world available to us.

Joginder Paul

On the Making of Fiction

JOGINDER PAUL

Joginder Paul (1925-2014) was born in Sialkot (now in Pakistan). His first story was published in the well-known Urdu journal 'Saqi' in 1945 while his first book of short stories in Urdu, Dharti ka Kaal *(Land Lust in English) was first published in 1962. The Partition of the country led to his migration to Ambala. His marriage led to another migration, to Kenya where he taught English, throughout expressing in his stories the angst of being in exile. Back in India in 1965, he was Principal of a college in Aurangabad, Maharashtra, for fourteen years before settling in Delhi for full-time writing.*

Paul published over 13 collections of short stories, including Khula, Khodu Baba ka Maqbara, *and* Bastian. *Amongst his novels are* EkBoond Lahoo ki, Nadeed, Paar Pare, *and* Khwabro. *He has four collections of flash fiction (Afsaanche), a genre with which he is known to have enriched Urdu fiction significantly. Most of his work has been published in Hindi as well. Many of his short stories and novels have been translated and published in English by National Book Trust, Penguin India, Katha and Harper Collins.*

Paul is a recipient of many literary honours including the SAARC Lifetime Award, Iqbal Samman, Urdu Academy Award, All India Bahadur Shah Zafar Award, Shiromani Award and the Ghalib Award.

He was also honoured at Doha with an Urdu Adab World award for contributing to creative writing in Urdu. His fiction has received critical acclaim and many Urdu journals in India and Pakistan have published special numbers on him.

SUKRITA: As a reader of your short stories, I consider your works 'modern' both in spirit and form. There is a certain sense of freedom in your fiction that does not seem to adhere to any fixed traditions of short story writing in Urdu. Nor does one get the impression that there are constraints in the choice of content you decide to present. Certainly commitment to the dictates of 'truth', as it were, is obvious. The reader follows the writer's lead in the story, until the moment of illumination is struck, and the truth of the situation comes home. The autonomy of the world of the short story is maintained convincingly which perhaps yields that experience of freedom to the reader. This is an important characteristic of modern writing. Of course, this freedom carries the burden of utmost responsibility, with which the writer explores the reality of the experience he chooses to write about. I'd like you to talk to me about the process through which an idea goes before it becomes a short story.

JOGINDER PAUL: When you ascribe responsibility to the freedom of the writer you acknowledge that pressures or rather some kinds of constraints are very much there. In one sense the writer is not free. But indeed the writer has to give himself any number of opportunities to reach a certain truth, no matter what path he may have to tread. However hazardous or uncomfortable this may be. Yes, he has to feel free to put his feet confidently on untrodden paths even if they start bleeding and hurting on the thorny, uncleared ways. Art has its own constraints. I remember once in a seminar on Global Consciousness at the Sahitya Akademi I spoke on how a writer does not really function with total freedom in the sense that he needs to *own* the local, specific truths of whatever he may have chosen to write on. Now supposing my concern is with an ant's journey from this end of the table to that, I need not be bothered then with global consciousness. I'd need to have an intimate, precise, and minute knowledge of the ant and its movements - that specific experience within that limited framework. I have to be master of that local experience. The same is true of freedom. It has, first and foremost, to go along with the limits of local truth of any experience itself.

We say so and so has written an 'original story' now, what's the meaning of 'original'? The word implies the essence of the story assumes its own native form. The writer has no choice but to discover that form. If he exercises his right to freedom irrespective of the genius of a story he may not be able to grasp the features unique to the story. He might also miss the opportunity to arrive at the truth specifically related to the story. Truth is always contextualized. There'd have to be adequate cognisance of the associative ideas which constitute the nucleus of the truth presented. It's very important in this discussion to point out the significance of the associative working of the creator. Therein no form is predefined. The short story by itself is such a form that, according to me, has no fixed shape or contours. There are as many ways of writing a short story as there are human beings. And, like a living being, a short story also has to appear to carry on its own independent existence. If the writer is able to come to grips with the original form of the story, the story moves creatively and rhythmically on its own and thus with perfect felicity. It assumes a bearing that grants little allowance for the platitudes or prejudices of the writer to hamper its original flow.

Some of our modern writers are, you see, sometimes obviously and irksomely deliberate in their choice of complex form, which they impose on their experience. This results in a painful disturbance in the authentic note of their writing. The strangest or, for that matter, most familiar of the literary forms would be in perfect tune if it originated from the story itself. It is perhaps like this; if you wore your native face, I should become familiar with you immediately on contact even though the face by itself were queer.

S: Since the traditions of 'katha', 'dastaan' etc. have been so firmly embedded in the Indian culture, the story writer here is bound to have preconceived ideas about what the form of his stories should be like. The 'modern' short story may use the existent traditions, but essentially it is a liberated art form. Do you think that the short story in Urdu and Hindi may have suffered because of the already existent traditions of storytelling? Or has writing in Hindi and Urdu gained from them?

JP: It's actually the preconceived ideas that undo the story. The writer has to keep himself open. If you meant this by freedom, then you were quite right. The writer has to arrive at the story through its own form. Preoccupation or unrelated preference in this regard may cripple his work. The thing will then remain in that state all its life...Of course, it is a matter of great responsibility to be able to carve out the story delicately and carefully, enough to retain the wholeness of the experience. A good writer's job is to get at the total figure by not breaking or chipping any part thereof. The story can very easily become a victim of his impatience. Or, it can also become a victim of clichés. What we call a great work is really a product of great patience and detachment. Sometimes a potentially great work falls short of greatness because the writer has torn it impatiently from his heart.

S: In many of your stories one notices that the characters are well-rooted in their cultural contexts. For instance,

"Bhabho"in your collection *Jadoo* is clearly the product of a specific section of society; similarly in "Dadiyan"you build up a specific cultural context in which the theme evolves. The situation is not abstractly universal. The totality is presented through observation of the minutely specific cultural context. It is as if the reader is observing along with the writer, and the universal or the elemental emerges through the specifics. On pondering over how this is achieved, I feel one stylistic feature which seems to have been used very effectively in some of your stories is the 'refrain'. For example in "Bhuk Pret"the refrain "khajoor to bahut meethi hai"(the dates are indeed very sweet). Now this line seems to be flowing constantly in the *witnessing* stream of consciousness of the character, which detaches the reader from the main action of the story. The reader is drawn into a point of identification with the main stream through a detailed narration of the specifics. But there's the other stream too, maintained by the refrain, that takes you away from the particulars and makes you transcend them even while being there.

JP: If you try and fit a refrain in every story extraneously it becomes a design ...

S: You do make use of this feature quite often ...

JP: Do I? ... But first let me explain. I'll tell you how and in which stories this feature appears. As I said, the habitual pursuit of a particular design makes a writer's oeuvre appear mannered. Of all my stories - of which there are so many - I have employed this device three or four times. In one case, in my short story "Baaz Deed"(The Second Look) – your appraisal is perhaps just. The iterative "That's all right" in the story becomes a little too loud and imposing. But in the other stories the refrain emerges naturally from situations apparently absurd. If you were to silence the refrain, you may run the risk of suppressing some of the essentials in those stories. The search necessary to grasp the absurd content of experience would naturally evolve a matching style. Where the refrain combines with the absurdity of the situation it creates a tickle, a very appreciative tickle. In my recent story "Gulzar"the Persian refrain "khushamadsheva je kuffar ast"(flatterers are infidels) is in accord with the absurdity and tempts the tickled reader to draw closer to the spirit of the story.

But then, if one starts using the refrain as discipline or a norm, then the repetition may fail to work and thus impede the freedom about which we were talking earlier. Within the framework of the story, wherever, whatever idiom is necessary and seems to come originally, I feel it swings me into action. But if I get onto a wrong track and employ the wrong idiom, the story seems to become stationary. Earlier, much more than now, before I actually managed to perceive the shape and contours of the story, I had had to struggle hard, occasionally unsuccessfully. But, nowadays, I seem to *hear* and feel the rhythm of the story even sooner than it makes its appearance to me. And when it has been located in the details of its face, the process of delivery sets in so organically, you may say, even without my interference. Another point: I think *specifics* are very important to the writing of a story normally but then this too is no strict norm. The importance of specific situations does not consist in their being material or concrete: they may emerge, if necessary, in a rather abstract way. Indeed, they help establish the authenticity of the story. A merely hypothetical story fails to involve the reader in its tension; even though it proves a point, he is not moved to identify himself with it in his everyday living as reference. The writer has to make the story live and pulsating, just as in a painting of a barren landscape, the barrenness too has to come alive for work to become art.

S: The artist, however, whether in writing a story or in painting, will have to discover a means to project his perspective one way or another. It's interesting to see a painter at work; one cannot see the story writer at work in the same way but I believe the creative consciousness would be working in the same way in both the cases. Well, what I am coming to particularly is the case of an abstract painting. The artist meticulously attempts to figure out the specifics even to create an abstract landscape. That happens in the presentation of some stories too, don't you think?

JP: As I said earlier, it's with the help of specifics that the experience gets established, authentically. It's strange that sometimes one's abstract stories may outwardly be rooted in a very material specific. For instance, my story "Peechhe". When the protagonist enters the sculptural habitat in the Ellora caves, he has a rather odd experience. Observing and mesmerized by the statues, he begins to feel that *he* is a statue and that the sculptured figures are observing him, not he them. The sense of wonder creates a statue of him. Now the situation presented is very material but the effect is so abstract.

S: If the approach had been hypothetical the idea would have been expressed and perhaps even explained but not experienced. The writer who can involve his reader into the expressed experience immediately is, I suppose, fortunate in having an appropriate craft.

Let us turn our attention to your major novel *Nadeed*. The novel records the spiritual malaise, the blindness, of people in contemporary times...The blindness of a people with open eyes! The degeneration of society into sloth, corruption, and darkness is all the more accentuated via the backdrop of its old values and ideals. Now, the west in the twentieth century has produced a whole gamut of social scientists, philosophers, and thinkers. Not so much here. A lot of intellectual fervour characterises our past, but in modern times there hasn't been much interaction between the intellectual and the artist as it was in the past. Maybe you'd like to comment on 'modern India.'

JP: One is affected by the way one actually chooses to live one's life. Are we living the way of our heritage? This is the pungent question. Today the whole world is flowing perhaps in a common stream and the reference to heritage is perhaps only an academic assumption. It's not enough just to get to know about something. *Mahabharat* and *Ramayana* are our heritage, but the truths of these epics come to us as mere second-hand knowledge. We have chosen to put that experience behind us.

Our present-day world has got so connected and so small that the east is no longer the east and the west no longer the west. There's been a whole lot of cultural give-and-take.

One's values develop in accordance with the style one actually lives. How are our values growing? We struggled so much for Independence before 1947. What were the dreams our people struggled, suffered, and sacrificed for? Haven't we lost track of the meaning of freedom? Today, apparently we are free, but for what and how?

It is possible that the earlier meanings of freedom are now irrelevant, but some verities can never be irrelevant. Which are those? While *Nadeed* deals on one level with the problems related to the Indian situation, on another level it's the story of our times all over the world. Whether or not a country is democratic, freedom on a certain plane has become a licence for a few dictators who prefer to pass as democrats. It's the state and quality of life lived by a whole people that matters. The story of *Nadeed* begins with a home for the blind, which keeps growing till the entire country looks like a house for the blind. Blindness here develops as a metaphor. We are looking but are unable to see, and, the person who's able to see claims that his eyes will keep seeing even after he's hanged and dead. He wants his eyes to be passed on to some blind man. But the blind does not accept his eyes, comprehending that the eyes would only be a noose around the neck. Now isn't that the problem of our times?

At one time the devil used to be painted with two canines jutting out of the mouth and one was able to recognize him at once as himself. Today if the devil has to be successful in his devilry he should look like a thorough gentleman. Where is his original identity then? Or what is the real identity of the gentleman today?

S: As the creator of intensely vital characters, you must have a wide range of vicarious experiences. To live life intensely on the one hand, and on the other to exist in the specific world of each of the short stories... what does this oscillation do to your state of mind? Are they two different planes of existence?

JP: A story does not become a work of art just by report: it has to actually happen to you. It's in this meaning that we talk of living stories. The Progressives at one time had started to say that the story is a medium for propaganda, while others have declared that art exists for art's sake alone. Both, according to me, are restrictively academic positions. I tell you at times in life I feel I'm in the process of writing a story; and, while I am writing a story, I cannot but feel I am actually going through the experience of it all. Oscillation would perhaps occur if creative writing were distinct from the experiences of life. There comes a stage in the life of a writer when he does not and cannot compartmentalize these experiences. He operates on the same plane and it is only then the writer acquires true creative capability. He then realizes' *the real* in his writing as well as outside it. The dividing line has to disappear for him to be able to discern and confront the authentic.

S: But in actual life, living amidst our rather hypocritical and pretentious middle-class society, one certainly does not have any control or freedom to operate in one's own way while,

I suppose, in the world of one's writings there'd be greater control...

JP: Hold, please. The other day I was reading somewhere about Narad Muni and Bhagwan watching a poor starving man dying. Now, Narad Muni impatiently tells Bhagwan, "Why don't you save that hapless character?" Here's the answer of Bhagwan: "I am Bhagwan! I cannot save him." A top-notch creative artist, God realizes that life sprouts in whatever shape from one's own *context and destiny,* and that even he must not interfere with the creative process. This may appear a contradiction, yet any in-depth study of the workings of nature will reveal how innumerable contradictions are reconciled to strike a balance.

S: As a creator, the writer attempts perhaps to grasp that essential characteristic of perceiving reconciliations and balance; the characters have to survive their inexorable truths.

JP: As in life, there's a sense of urgency in a work of art. A piece of writing that's hypothesized rather than experienced lacks direness, urgency, and quite often fails to evoke the tension so necessary to involve both the writer and the reader. To see what I mean, think of the world's greatest short stories. It's for the crisis and inevitability they generate that they are unforgettable...

S: As a writer how do you perceive 'time', while in the process of writing, especially when in real life, time consciousness remains linear?

JP: A story occurs sometimes in such peculiar circumstances that you may not quite identify it in the first instance. An idea suddenly creeps in from one's long-lost past and the writer, if he can place it, ties it up with something from the present. You see, when one is actually living, life presents itself day after day, week after week, year after year - that's the experience of the non-written linear life. But after one has lived through years and years of it, all of it can be recalled in a second. It is clear that the writer does not just 'expose' the pastness of such experiences. It is its appearance in the present that the artist has to grasp.

S: So to a writer, totally submerged in creative experience, all time is available at once and the approach to time is not linear. Everything of the past is immediately accessible and whatever is situationally relevant is picked up naturally and inevitably in the present. The contours of the story get defined alongside.

JP: I believe that till such a moment as everything - your experience, life, past and present, the inside and the outside of the story - merge into one organic whole in whatever time scheme, there cannot be creative activity. The important thing is to have the capacity to go through it as a genuine experience.

S: There arises another related question... when such awareness is available to one and when you are living as well as writing creatively…

JP: Well, that stage comes when it does, and one is indeed fortunate if it does come...

S: But along with that a whole range of problems of practical living would emerge because modern living after all calls for a rather mechanized lifestyle. A sensitive awareness of the goings-on in one's everyday life can turn one cynical or an absurdist or it may just lead one to a very insular living. It may create an acute sense of loneliness as well, as establishing communication may be a serious problem. The gap between the sensitive artist and the society in which she's operating is very wide. Have you ever felt that you've had to change your mode of communication because you are not reaching your society or that you are either not understood at all or are misunderstood?

JP: This poses a very important question - why does

one write at all? For success or for suffering? Why resort to creative writing? Creative writing necessarily implies a sort of communication which predisposes the writer's involuntary urge to suffer for all his fellow-beings. It may sound tragic that the poor fool has to live in and through all his characters and not be himself. He could not become everybody unless he himself were nobody. So, he poses no problem to himself; his problems consist of others', including those of all the villains and the vamps. He himself is the killer he chooses to portray. He doesn't *judge* the killer. He becomes him and owns his sins. It's in this sense that creative writing is regarded as confessional. A writer choosing to operate 'successfully' in his society will be one of those who withdraw, judge and condemn, not those who are condemned - No! No, please! Let the writer remain misunderstood and disturbed.

S: How do you manage to escape all those problems which may have pulled you away from the main track of creativity as you define it?

JP: Oh, you learn to fall into the rhythm by and by. But to tell you the truth, I do not escape the problems. I pass through them, as I have suggested, as a nobody. And, since I do not exist, the problems fail to notice me. Even a snake will venture to bite you only when it knows you are somebody. You have to dodge, you know, even when you are most well-intentioned. Yet, to be very honest, I do sometimes ask myself, what is more important, to live my writing or my life? What's more native to man, living originally or doing original writing? I do not know the answer except that I salute both who live originally and who are original writers. Both are artists. Yes, even the writers. Because they wouldn't be original unless they lived their writing. I fervently believe that the writer as a human being and as a writer cannot be two different beings.

Unless he is used to treating his writing with as much

concern as he does his personal deeds, he cannot imbue it with breath, life, and urgency. And if he appears different from his writing it only means that either his writing is false or the contradiction is merely seeming and the observer has not been able to reconcile it with the writer's inwardness. As I suggested earlier, all his truths are with reference to his literary context: locally universal. As a writer he cannot but be faceless. In my meaning, personally identityless.

S: So why does one write at all?

JP: I believe everybody writes: some by teaching in a classroom or working in a laboratory; some by shop-keeping, some by cobbling; some by reading; and some of course by writing. Whatever way or field you seek to express yourself sensitively in becomes your natural medium of expression. Self-expression is inborn in every living entity and it's the measure of the passion with which a person pursues his medium that makes an artist of him. Baba Nanak has said that even the vilest of human beings contains somewhere in him the creator himself. I unreservedly subscribe to this view.

S: What happens when you finish a story? Do you get a sense of fulfilment? Or do you feel restless that there's so much more to explore and express?

JP: Well it's like this; you are always in a state of waiting, waiting for the story you have not yet been able to write. You go on waiting story after story, each so dear to you, but the story you have ever waited for remains unwritten.

You pass away, still waiting for the unwritten story. And this unwritten story is perhaps written by someone in the next generation. What one calls the continuing relevance of the creative writer is nothing but the awareness of his successors: what more he could have done, the works that remained unwritten and can now be written when he is no more. Thus does a creative writer strive for his fulfilment. He knows his own limitations but he also perceives the unlimitedness of life he represents. Intentionally or no, he inspires the generation in the wings to take its cue from him.

S: Your medium of expression is the word. To be able to use any medium for creative purposes, I suppose, there's got to be intense faith in it. Have you ever felt that language is inadequate for the purpose of creative communication?

JP: Words, I think, become terrible traps and constraints if you regard them as significant by themselves. The adventure of a parade of exclusive words in glittering uniform only serves to jam the traffic in literature. Words have to function wordlessly to have an enduring life-like impact. It may appear paradoxical, but communicative words recreate a scene silently, as in a picture. The greater the artistic felicity of the writer over a quiet use of words, the less the apprehension that language is inadequate for creative communication.

S: Yes, but don't you occasionally feel frustrated by language, your tool, to express your experience?

JP: It depends. I experienced the predicament in "Gulzar", the story I mentioned earlier, and at the fag end of another story, "Aage Peechey". Sometimes your experience is perhaps too profound for language. If on this occasion language doesn't also become the inward experience, you are likely to feel unhinged. And any deliberateness on your part is more likely to lead you away from the moment, that overwhelming moment. I should tell you a story here: a fellow writer had been forever using a volley of words to express his profound and subtle thoughts. When he died at this juncture, another writer remarked, "I can understand him more fully now, in his effortless, permanent silence than in all his strenuous speech."

S: Can a story writer avoid being deliberate?

JP: Perhaps he can't; but I am one with Chekov who believes a story on the surface level of art should never *betray* its writer's deliberate intention to the reader.

S: You have compared the experience of meditation, of a yogi, with that of art in the context of both aiming at some realization of truth and owning as well as absorbing larger reality.

JP: Have you heard of the old Greek maxim, "Hard is the beautiful"? Both yoga and art are very very exacting. Not forbiddingly exacting, for they engage you into and out of routine, in spite of yourself. I am not a yogi; but as an artist I have always felt intrigued by the intuitive and direct experiences of a yogi or a darvesh. Before attainment, a darvesh passes through a life-long self-imposed training to figure existence out, in its exact proportions, and to search for the divine rhythm underlying existence. So what appears to be spontaneous inspiration should also point, upon maturity, and as in the case of an artist, to years and years of devout and involved training. But for an intimacy with and resultant grip over the mechanics of creative activity you may fail to experience life directly and intuitively. Behind intuitiveness works - I'm sure it does work - your capacity to identify a balance between frenzy and the mechanics of creative activity, and of course, you enjoy all this so essentially. In point of fact it's your faculty to enjoy the discovery of the balance that makes you feel you have just intuitively discovered it. Well, whatever! But the balance has to be created and maintained the same way as it is in nature herself.

S: There are a whole lot of personal experiences that one has in one's life. And then many a writer, as you do in your own short stories, recall those past experiences. What is this need to go back to them? Is it that those experiences linger because there may be a sense of unfulfillment about them? Is there an effort to detach one's self from them through art?

JP: First, the meaning of 'personal' experience has to

be clarified. When one is writing, one does not narrate those experiences as they were actually lived by one. In the organic whole of what you are writing, that specific experience demands a different pattern, in synthesis. Whether the experience is acquired through someone else or directly, it modifies itself in accord with a different situation and its own unity in the new context. The new truths, local to this unity, have to be conformed with. Old experiences then get moulded in a new framework. If the exact expression of the recalled experience is attempted the product will be a mere report, perhaps an impassioned report, but not art. And that would be rife with the writer's prejudices, petty concerns, platitudes…

S: Does the experience of reliving your own life through your writing have a cathartic effect?

JP: Yes and no! Not necessarily, because as long as one is alive and similarly involved, recurrence of old memories may bring back deeper pain which, of course, you have greater capacity at this stage to put up with!

S: The modern short story makes great use of metaphors, symbols, allegories, and other literary devices. How do you approach them theoretically?

JP: Critics talk a great deal of the use of metaphors, symbols etc. Rules are worked out and abstractions sorted, as if their use were a formal exercise. A situation itself can sometimes become a metaphor in its entirety, as in Manto's story "Khol Do". I regard it as a perfect metaphor, for it cannot be torn apart from the context. What I am driving at is that there are no hard and fast rules with which to work out a conscious use of devices in a short story. The story itself should dictate its means and how they evolve appropriately. The 'modern' uses of symbols, abstractions, absurdities, allegories and the like are quite compatible with the complexities of our times, yet the means by themselves do not explain the modern appeal of a short story. As discussed earlier, a short story must form all its features naturally, from its own seedling. No story can really be significant just because it is symbolic, allegorical, or abstract: it has to be its own self to sustain interest. If some mannerism or device gets used and exhibited merely to 'win' modernist credentials, art becomes restrictive and contrived.

S: What would you say about Kafka's *Metamorphosis* in this context?

JP: Kafka in *Metamorphosis* is superb: the incredible absurd in the story is perfectly in tune with the inward reality of modern man, shown to be *actually* living his steady metamorphosis into a gigantic cockroach.

S: Our critical scene seems to be trapped in borrowed critical terminology. What is excellent in art hardly gets critically examined with indigenous critical tools. Some critics become power-brokers while creative writing seems to be flourishing in an isolated domain. Does this affect you or disturb you in any way?

JP: Fortunately for the writer, the reader has first to approach the writer direct. Even the critic would only be true in his critical appraisals if, first and foremost, he were just a reader. Judgement, though necessary, is by itself rather mean. The judge, however, is redeemed when he is inclined to partake of and thus share the suffering of the creative activity he wishes to adjudge. As for your impressions of the current critical scene, yes, the state of affairs is disturbing enough. But writers should, therefore, be bolder, freer and much more forthright. Moreover, dependence on criticism, even honest criticism can only make a first-rate writer too cautious. To be a true creative writer one has to confidently depend upon one's own perceptions and insights. Siddartha in Hesse's *Siddartha* justly refused to abide by the Buddha's teachings. To obtain nirvana, he would rather go by what he himself truly went through. The nirvana of a writer also rests on how freely he expresses what he actually passes through and discerns. But then it would be interesting to know how the fraternity of trained critics respond to what the writer creates, as compared to the general reader…

S: Perhaps that will be our subject through yet another discussion session. Thanks very much for the story of creativity, inside out.

Namwar Singh

On Modernism in Hindi

NAMWAR SINGH

Born in 1927, *educated in Varanasi, NAMWAR SINGH began his literary career writing poetry and literary essays. He became famous (and infamous!) for his willingness to court controversy, and explore ideas across ideological spectra – but his staunchest critics agree that his literary credentials, his capacities as a teacher, and his scholarship are practically unparalleled. Namwar Singh has taught literature at* Banaras *Hindu University, Jodhpur University, and eventually in Jawaharlal Nehru University, where he headed the Centre of Indian Languages and remainsed till the end, Professor Emeritus. His contribution to literary criticism in Hindi is well-acknowledged – his essay on modernism is taught in translation across departments of English as well as of modern Indian languages across universities. Editor of the Hindi critical quarterly* Alochana, *he has written several books on modern Hindi literature, the* nayi kahani *(new story), and poetry in Hindi. For his book,* Kavita Ke Naye Pratiman *he was awarded the Sahitya Akademi Award.*

SUKRITA: I would like to begin this discussion on the modern Hindi short story by invoking the concept of modernism. Should we not distinguish between 'modernism' as it emerged in the west in 20th century English literature and modernism as it was received or evolved in the context of Hindi literature? European modernism can perhaps be seen as a crisis of western civilization earlier in the century. It acquired the tone of rigorous questioning of the established ideas, a philosophic probe, and a scientific and rational examination of faith and religion that transformed society. Literature produced around this time demonstrated the fragmented human psyche in its varied and new forms. Conventional forms seemed inadequate for the creative expression of such a sensibility. A similar modernist temper seems to emerge about three decades later in the post-Premchand Hindi short story. What cultural crisis do you think explains the concern for formalistic innovation and new perspectives in Hindi literature of the times? Is this an imitative modernism, a mere borrowing ...a kind of a colonial hangover?

NAMWAR SINGH: Well, I look at modernism as an experience. You are right: we see this in the early twentieth century in the west, around World War I. There was a social transformation then. The temper of the age prescribed a semi-industrialist, semi-scientific approach. The labour movement added to concern about development. Actually, I would call it semi-development, because English society's quasi-aristocratic bearing could not easily accept the displacement of the old and the established. The questioning of religion could not be tolerated easily either. And so one notices a reaction.... Eliot and Pound and some others were highly critical of the modern, technology-oriented society. And of course, one knows about the championing of primitivism in D.H. Lawrence...

S: So, do you see reaction as inherent to modernism?

N S: Well, it is this *experience* of *reaction*, and then acceptance, followed by rejection of the transformation in sensibility that I call modernism. The critical stance towards 'modern elitist' society too can already be discerned. Eliot references organic, pre-Miltonic society, before the 'dissociation of sensibility'. Donne, in that context, must be considered a 'modern' poet. In our literature however, the modernist movement becomes visible in the early forties – in Hindi poetry much earlier than in prose.

S: And would you say it was western modernism that effectively entered our literature?

NS: I'd say that in the thirties, our writers were taking to modernism ideologically. There was a powerful trend towards 'progressive writing' that abetted the freedom struggle, but the concern for development was more or less theoretical. That was one kind of modernism; literature being created in an ideological frame. Eliot's modernism certainly created new waves of thought in literature the world over. But again, in our own country circumstances change after independence. There was a planned movement towards industrialization, an organized, pragmatic preoccupation with science and technology. Lots of stories and novels were being written with a new enthusiasm. However, the experience of modernism as I define it emerged in the writings of writers such as Phanishwar Renu who reacted *against* urbanization by depicting only rural characters in a village setting. The pull towards the 'real' and the rural on the one hand, and, the concern for 'progress' on the other–that is what I see as the Indian literary experience of modernism.

S: Are the English intellectual debates on tradition and modernity through the first quarter of the twentieth century relevant to Indian society later in the fifties, do you think? I'm going back to your point about two kinds of modernism in Hindi literature...

NS: I think the first, 'progressive writing' kind of

modernism did not involve much of Anglicization. In the latter case the impact of the English language and literature is quite obvious. The imagery and symbols are sometimes directly borrowed. I think the spirit of innovation and experimentation witnessed earlier declined later on, in the fifties.

S: Why do you think the hard-won independence did not inspire confidence and a certitude in the person of the Indian subject? Shouldn't there have been a fearless owning of one's culture, myths, and archetypes that helped evolve a distinct 'native' and 'authentic' Indian identity? Would you say there is evidence of an assertion of indigenous identity in the post-Independence Hindi short story? Also, has there been a dearth of intellectual engagement and philosophical probing in sorting out new values and beliefs? In the west, Nietszche, Marx, Sartre and so many other intellectual giants kept up with a philosophical quest, provoking discussions and debates on the perception of reality throughout the century...Surely Gandhi should have had a similar impact on the Indian psyche? But the Indian intellectual or writer seemed more under the influence of Sartre or Marx. In the late sixties or perhaps the seventies, an identifiable modern Hindi short story begins to take shape – I mean that a clearly Indian voice seems to evolve...

NS: Perhaps we could go a little deeper into the question of why the post-Independence Indian subject should lack self-confidence. We must think about how we got Independence – the really hard way! And nobody expected the country to be divided. The partition of the country shocked and traumatised everyone.

S: The phenomenon of partition benumbed the nation, and its literature?

NS: Yes, certainly. The communal riots, the holocaust, overpowered any joy that freedom from the British could have brought. That is why you find so many novels and stories that take partition or the riots as their theme. There was no stability for at least five, six years in the country. It was a state of absolute upheaval.

Thousands of people were displaced, and refugee culture cast a sad shadow over the country. You mentioned Gandhi. We cannot forget he was murdered, and I think all of Gandhian culture was murdered with him... Those values were shattered. And rather than confidence, there was a spirit of diffidence. Look at the short story of the fifties and sixties. You'll find that lots of writers, including Renu, presented two generations of characters: an elder who upheld the glory of the past and a younger striving to cope with the depressing complexity of the present. Many stories referred to the reality of prior times through one or two representative characters belonging to that generation juxtaposed with the young. This emphasized the contrast between the pre-modern and the now. In fact from Premchand onwards there is an obvious streak of *primitivism* in Hindi fiction...

S: But would it be correct to say that the experience of modernism as you term it took root in India and found indigenous creative expression, say in the sixties and seventies?

NS: Our late-thirties modernism was much less of an experience. It was more of an intellectual exercise. It seeped into our culture gradually and evolved into a real Indian experience long after Independence.

S: Regarding the critical perception or understanding of post-Independence writing– I wonder why there seems hardly any discernible identification of a collective literary *movement* by critics? Each great writer seems a category unto her or himself. In English literature on the other hand, despite a rather amorphous conception of modernism fiction writers are grouped into specific schools of thought, some common critical perspectives are worked out and the dominant trends

–Expressionism, Naturalism, Impressionism, Symbolism, etc.–are named. Why do you think critical approaches to Hindi fiction avoid such categorization? Is it that the literature itself does not call for it?

NS: For one, we do not see specific movements as such in modern Hindi fiction. There aren't any schools of thought around which a whole lot of writing may have been done. In a single writer you see many tendencies, varied, alongside each other. In that the writer in himself is a school of thought – yes, a category unto himself. For instance, the way Nirmal Verma would write, only he could write. A Kashinath Singh will not have other writers of the same sensibility around him. Also I think Hindi critics have been in a way apathetic, not involved enough. They seem to have found an easy way out, using the "period" concept for critical convenience - the post-fifties story, or the post-sixties story... No doubt the period concept helps the critic trace historicity. But I think the critic needs to analyse the work or experience of a writer more deeply to identify the dominant currents. Then perhaps common features could be worked out. The Hindi story of the time is not perceived as potentially reflective of specific conceptualizations at all.

S: Does the paucity of critical approaches affect literary standards among readers? And are university departments making efforts to sort out critical norms and standards?

NS: Not at all. In the west, criticism is perpetually developing. University departments become centres of criticism, in which critical approaches are evolved. In our case literature departments seem to be limited to teaching syllabi and examination. Perhaps one reason why modern literature is not popular is that there is no live involvement in what's been currently happening in literature. There are old, established ideas which are conveniently handed down from one generation to the next without any critical review. There is in fact a clear aversion to modern literature...perhaps because it involves fresh thinking and a different orientation. I'd say that the role of universities in literary criticism at present is that they have none.

S: While going through one of your interviews recently published in a journal, I came across a comment made by you on the short stories of Shashank. You have said that Shashank's short stories hardly evoke a response in you. That you are not sure whether you'd like to call that form a short story at all. Could you elaborate?

NS: Perhaps it's my own limitation rather than the author's. But this young writer doesn't seem aware of what exactly he wants to say. The form that he uses is extremely fluid or amorphous and sometimes there is an utter inadequacy of content matter. I feel rather upset when the story fails to convey the writer's intention. It is of course much worse when the writer gives the impression of not being able to understand his own intention. There are other writers of Shashank's generation who seem to practice a similar vein of creative expression; somehow I can't respond to it.

S: Could you compare it with the impressionistic style of Alain Robbe-Grillet, where images are used without the writer's mediation? I mean signification of the images is avoided, for instance in his novel *Jealousy*? The technique used is such that jealousy comes across to the reader without the writer identifying it...The form is cinematic, the pattern subterranean.

NS : I am familiar with the writings of this French novelist, and I do enjoy his fiction despite its abstraction. But there is a distinct point-of-view integral to the technique. In our recent stories I notice a tendency to experiment with the form without any definable point-of-view. And that is what I am not able to appreciate. I feel that even today the Hindi writer is much more comfortable with the realist tradition. At most he has successfully used the journalistic style, or reportage, also in vogue in the west through the past few years.

S: Is it true that more convincing short stories are being written in Urdu than in Hindi. Can one account for this difference? I'd say the sensibilities ought to be close and that the linguistic and narrative expression therefore would match each other.

NS: Urdu has a more prominent storytelling tradition. And from Saadat Hasan Manto to Ismat Chughtai to the present lots of short stories seem to share a 'modern' sensibility. Joginder Paul, for instance, has written very good stories but how many new writers have the same confidence? I don't really think there is a significant difference between the Hindi and the Urdu literary scenes.

S: A conscious movement towards 'impersonality' can be traced in English literature through the later twentieth century... Yeats used the 'mask', and marionette theatre has been used to create distance between the word and the person uttering it. I mean the earlier twentieth-century concern for the self or the 'individual' is no longer the primary theme. If, for instance, the story revolves around a woman-character, it is not the individual identity which preoccupies the writer; it is the 'woman' as a phenomenon. Is there such a trend in Hindi, too?

NS: No, I don't think so. I think the new feature is the emergence of lots of women writers in Hindi, though –some of them exceptional, committed writers – Raji Seth, Mrinal Pande, Manjul Bhagat...

S: Which is indeed a positive note to wind up on! Thank you very much!

Muhammad Ali Siddiqui

On Modernism in Urdu Fiction

MUHAMMAD ALI SIDDIQUI

MUHAMMAD ALI SIDDIQUI, (1938-2013), *perhaps best known as* Dawn *newspaper's literary and critical columnist* Ariel, *was born in India and migrated with his family to Karachi in 1948. He served as President of the Progressive Writers' Association, Pakistan, and was a valued member of several distinguished international literary bodies. He wrote sixteen original full-length books (including* Tawazun, *which won Best Book of the Year as well as Best Book of Urdu Criticism in 1976, and* Croce ki Sarguzasht, *awarded in 1979), over a hundred articles, and lectured at universities in Karachi, London, Oslo, Toronto, and Ottawa. Siddiqui earned a D.Litt. in Pakistan Studies and an MA in English literature; he was a polyglot who knew French, Persian, Punjabi, Sindhi, and Seraiki as also, Urdu and English (in addition to conducting surveys in Pashtu and Brahui). He held a variety of high-level editorial, faculty and educational-administrative posts, and is remembered as one of the most astute, nuanced, and erudite scholars of northwestern subcontinental modernisms to emerge out of 20th century Pakistan.*

SUKRITA: With reference to the specific turn of the century literary movement termed modernism in the west, I would like to focus your attention on post-independence Urdu literature of India and Pakistan. Writers here have been 'modernist' too. But what is their relation to the specific historical and cultural factors leading to the movement in the west termed literary modernism, that seemed to have risen from the cultural crisis between the two world wars? I wish to understand the modernism witnessed in the Indian subcontinent in relation to the impact of this movement on a culture which is radically so different. Can ideas, in such a circumstance, be transplanted and do we eventually have an indigenous concept of modernism emerging in the literatures of our countries?

MUHAMMAD ALI SIDDIQUI: Of course, there's been a definite impact of the western modernist wave. But there is also truth in the statement that by and by we have evolved our own indigenous concept. It is like economic development. With economic development, changes occur through society, and society has to catch up with the requirements of the economic development. Some notions of the cosmopolitan creep in. Even in the nineteenth century a lot of modern notions became part of our psyche. Initially we rejected these ideas since they seemed mere appendages of the British Raj, but even revolutionaries such as Raja Ram Mohan Roy, Bankim Chandra Chatterjee, and Indian National Congress leaders like Jawaharlal Nehru eventually welcomed modernism, because modernism meant progress, development, and there arose the hope of eradicating backwardness and poverty. At times western ideas were modified to suit our own condition. Yes, the progress of modernity in the east is very different from that in the west. In the west, modernism was in certain ways a reaction against democracy and enlightenment. It is strange but it happened so! In one of his essays Roger Fry wrote that when democracy was introduced in France in 1870, all the monarchists turned towards symbolism and became modernists. It was he who coined the term 'modernists' to distinguish them from the 'moderns'. The modernist became one who opted for a state of withdrawal and did not wish to face reality or be concretely grounded.

S: Do you think this is echoed in our own literatures?

MAS: Well, in this subcontinent, modernism was synonymous with notions of progress... We needed an infrastructure. Railways, for instance, became the biggest public sector undertaking to unite the subcontinent...

S: But in the context of literature and aesthetics, and modernism followed by postmodernism – these seemed to be branching out of some fresh notions and literary features. The modernists here took on experimentalism along with a collapse of the conventional form and experienced a crisis while seeking to locate their identity. A general atmosphere of uncertainty and scepticism seeped into the literary sensibility... Philosophers such as Nietzsche, Darwin, and others had reconsidered crucial questions about human life and offered ideas that questioned certainties upheld by the western world for centuries, for instance Nietzsche's declaration of the "death of God" that shook the 'faith' on which all security of human existence rested. With such social and philosophical upheaval in the western world, there was an obvious transformation in the sensibility of man. Can we view 'modernism' here within this framework too? Would you comment on the impact it might have had on our literature?

MAS: There is no doubt that the nineteenth century was a century of definite ideas about the universe. The root of confusion, I think, lies in the identification of 'modernism' – which I maintain has to be seen differently in the east and the west. As for experimentalism - well, what impels the writer to seek new forms? Some writers found that traditional forms were not adequate and were not helping them to express reality any more. And so the ready acceptance of anything new – here the new that came from the west. I recall Marx's comment from one of his despatches to the *New York Tribune* –he welcomes the British Raj in India, disliking, of course, their method of grabbing power. He was perhaps thinking of industrialization, democracy, nationalism, and the tremendous inflow of European ideas and scholarship into India. Writers in the subcontinent were well aware of Gogol, Maupassant, and Turgenev. In Bengal particularly, there was a concrete awareness. Traditional writers could liberate themselves of the constraints of conventional form and new ideas were absorbed in their writing through the means of new forms. But this is crucial – the indigenous notion of the modern included love for progress and love for freedom while most western modernists did not like populist views and looked down on all those who clamoured for freedom or socialism. So the philosophical basis of modernism in the east necessarily acquired shades distinctly different from those of the west. So we ultimately gained a lot from the process of accepting modernism as a liberating force. It did wonders for literature.

S: Liberation from traditional art forms through 'new' ones also evokes the transplantation of ideas from across the continent. The western modernist practiced formal innovation in realization of the change in sensibility. Experimentalism has to be related to what it seeks to do. Ideas and concepts flowed in to the subcontinent with western education and influence. They needed to be modulated and given shape with a craving for free expression unprecedented in centuries of literary production. How did we adjust these ideas within the context of our steadfast old values? These traditions have persisted to date. We have preserved some 'certainties' about human existence, rational or irrational. Have we enjoyed the advantages of both the worlds… Resting on the bounty of a rich heritage, exposing ourselves uninhibitedly to the west. The nature of this fresh awareness should have yielded rich and meaningful literary experiences, perhaps even more meaningful than the transient, ephemeral expression of a change in western sensibility... Do you think we have adequately sorted out a critical basis that might take this exciting difference into account? Have we satisfactorily attempted critical examinations of the impact of western ideas, our adjustments and the extent of their absorption in our literatures?

MAS: I think this is a very interesting situation. Some of the 'moderns' in India and Pakistan have been able to absorb western modernism and realign or reconfigure it in accordance with local contexts. Some on the other hand are quite medieval and obscurantist. I have always wondered what really makes them so. Going back to the past and staying there only avoids the present. There is an effective use of the shifting past and present, the movement of the author in time and space through the use, say, of techniques like stream of consciousness – as in the case of Qurratulain Hyder's *Aag Ka Darya.* Such beautiful use of history in fiction! No, I don't think there is a theory of modernism to be prescribed to subcontinental 'moderns'. To me modernism is an extension of romanticism, as opposed to classicism, where the 'we' is very significant. Even when a writer sought individual artistic expression, she in fact confronted the whole age and projected a sense of history.

S: Though a specificity of the 'I' emerges in modern literature, I would have thought the artistic expression of confrontation, of individual self with 'objective' experience, is as representative an expression of the classicist as of the ... But as a reader one surely feels a paucity of critical thinking – subcontinental modernisms don't have a body of critical norms or clearly delineated evaluative modes to refer to. Scattered and diffused thinking cannot really help build a critical tradition. The aim is to identify modernist literature, which is simultaneously modern and perpetual.

MAS: There are some who've emerged from restrictive critical domains: Wazir Agha, Shamsur Rehman Farooqui, and also perhaps Intezar Husain. Some of the writers are modern and progressive; some are modern and retrogressive. Not only do they manifest a desire to postpone the confrontation with the present, they also want to revert to an Indo- version of an Arcadian past. They may have fine reconstructive skills but the approach seems also to negate the present.

S: Is it an effort to work out universals? I mean to see how far the past is relevant or how one can reinterpret the past? Their success would, of course, depend on how successful they are in painting the archetypal.

MAS: Intezar Husain is a great artist no doubt, but he perpetuates notions that don't really 'sit well' with modernity. Glamorization of certain traditionalist notions and romanticization of, say, the bullock cart, I would regard that type of thing as a deliberate effort to nullify the achievements of the modern age that begin to appear almost obsolete again. It propagates a nostalgia that retards progress or forward thinking. We do appreciate ideas that liberalize or secularize, especially given the current climate. Writers who confuse modernism with mere barrenness could themselves be bracketed as obscurantists.

Some who want to be regarded as moderns may not really be modern. If there is some confusion, it is in their aesthetic and historical framework, not ours. The use of western techniques, of movement in time and space, like the use of any innovative techniques to facilitate expression, is good in itself. It is important to realize the historical limits of one's language and its literary traditions and seek to expand its and their scope. If my literary traditions do not permit a full expression of my experience I should feel free to go to other literatures for a suitable device and incorporate it, enhancing my own language and its literature.

S: Only, we need to exercise caution so as not to merely superimpose a technique onto one's individual or cultural expression; the writer needs to own the device in such a way that it becomes one with the context of her or his experience.

MAS: Ninety per cent of my critical writings through my first book *Tawazum* and the second one *Nishanaat* deal with this point. I have been very critical of the blind imitation of western techniques without any appreciation for what made a Joyce or a Yeats. We can't have repeat-performances in literature. But then criticism can only point out and be candid or even unkind; it can't check. Those who are engaged in imitating without insight or any philosophic basis will ultimately insult the reader.

S: And in a way they also demonstrate a loss of self-respect...

MAS: If the author does not own her or his experience, how will the reader accept it! But I think such work dies a quick death. It does not last long. Though of course I can understand impatience in persons like yourself...

S: But Ali sahib, my own reaction is not just against such writers but also against the critic who is not forthright and unbiased in her or his approach. I don't mean that the critic can guide the writer, but she can certainly help create a suitable readerly environment for the acceptance or critique of literary works. Our criticism needs to carry the responsibility of its discipline.

MAS: Critics are just clearing houses. It's appalling to witness the kind of insensitivity demonstrated by some critics in our languages. Bland imitations have been termed 'modern'. The obvious symptoms of existential awareness, a product of the explosion of knowledge, say between 1880 and 1910, emerged also as feelings of boredom and a sense of futility. To use these reactive impressions of life in an altogether different culture is rather naive. With the Second World War there was another realignment of ideology in the west.

A shifting and adjustment of new ideas and a consequent intellectual chaos was witnessed. Our modern intellectual usually imbibes ideas from Europe directly or is indirectly subject to a Pan-European influence. I think MIT's (Massachusetts Institute of Technology) strategy was to deprive the intellectual of any romance, any dream of restructuring systems in accordance with new times, and to actually rebuild society in a more collective way. On the other hand most of our intellectuals became individual prophets of doom and death. That's why the work of some progressive writers with modern ideas acts like dynamite blasting the whole facade of writing that does not confront reality. On an ideological plane the latter holds no water.

S: Would you say that the form of the modern short story is itself a western import? Though we have long cherished the old tradition of *kath a* and *dastaan* here, the modern short-story has acquired an altogether different shape and colour. Many a modernist critic here is concerned with whether the subcontinental modern short story is a story at all.

This debate is particularly relevant to us, within the context of our own ancient forms. Would you like to offer a comment on the short story?

MAS: A short story is an opportunity for the reader to relive the writer's mood. The short story writer should say something either to make the reader share insights about a character or about a particular moment. He has to do all he can to make it work. The author is free to use what devices he wants to. He might use 'plot' for instance or may totally eliminate it. Some stories may be highly poetic, others may be classically well-knit. And some may be monologues. The important thing is that it should have a powerful impact. The form is a very fluid one and the writer has to very carefully select technique and style and then present experience in an effective and wholesome manner with as keen an eye to aesthetic restraints as any classicist.

S: Perhaps it's a question of some intrinsic harmony - whether that harmony is struck or not. The logic of the form has to be woven in with the content. Once the writer is able to organically establish the inner harmony, perhaps the question whether it is a 'short story or not' becomes irrelevant?

MAS: In terms of writerly honesty and integrity Saadat Hasan Manto is exemplary. He remains a great writer even today for the sheer honesty of purpose projected through his artefacts. Krishan Chander's work, considered as an omnibus too presents the complications and tensions of his age directly. The master's hand should lie concealed in his art – the apparently artless manner of an artwork becomes all the more effective through the creator's meticulous planning and care. If a writer does not give me a chance to react or feel my consciousness expand, I as a reader will not be able to entertain him either. I'd like to give examples here of some contemporary writers who have done marvels in the art of storytelling: Surendra Prakash has one such story, Balraj Manra and Anwar Sajjad a few, and of course Joginder Paul has many short stories which do not remain mere stories; they yield an awareness in which all of a sudden the insides of man and his existence lie exposed, illuminating all that has been taken for granted.

S: The reader's experience of discovery is simultaneous with a sense of familiarity. The reader partakes of the author's creative adventure.

MAS: And human sensitivity is enhanced through such experiential contacts, yes. A short story aims at the reader's total involvement, to the point of complete identification with the exploration of a view. A reader may arrive at a different conclusion from that offered by the writer, may hang very different meanings to the experience. But the open-ended short story becomes all the more exciting thus and has a life-like existence layered with probabilities and possibilities. And so too the many-layered meanings and interpretations acquire validity. How can one, in this context, propound theories of what modernism is? Theories would be mere straitjackets in which creativity would be stifled.

S: But one does imagine that an authentic critical examination of modern artworks would help sort out the good from the bad. Modernism should not be used as a licence for licentiousness in art.

MAS: Lack of certain training, in agility of mind, is perhaps to blame for the absence of a critical tradition in India and Pakistan. The critic should certainly try to perform the role of reformer, of literary taste. Of late some stress has been laid on the issues raised by you. For instance, modern Urdu fiction is being taken seriously for the first time, and some critics have wakened to the challenge.

S: That indeed is a hopeful note to end with! Thank you.

Wazir Agha

On Modernity in Urdu Fiction

WAZIR AGHA

Sitara-e-Imtiaz WAZIR AGHA (1922-2010) was a distinguished poet and critic – particularly known for his essays, poems and humour in contemporary Urdu literature. Editor of Auraq, *a leading Pakistani Urdu-language literary journal, he contributed immensely to creating a distinctly modern critical and creative climate in Urdu literature through his own writing, through his generous and expansive mentorship of hundreds of writers over a six-decade career, as a writer and through his journal. Translations of his poetical works into English include* The Evening and Shadows, The Yellow Mountain of the Day, Half a Century Later, *and* Butterflies in the Grass. Stray Thoughts and the Other End, *one of his many collections of essays, is also available in English. His critical works include* Satire and Humour in Urdu Poetry *and* The Native Genius of Urdu Poetry. *Settled in Sargodha, Pakistan, Wazir Agha was as unassuming as the farmers on his land in Wazir Kot, where he spent most of his time. A thorough scholar, Wazir Agha was well aware of sophisticated critical stances from all over the world.*

I had the good fortune of meeting him for a conversation before he passed away in Lahore, Pakistan.

SUKRITA: Agha Sahib, you've been a great exponent of what is called 'modern literature' and are recognized as one of the stalwarts of modern Urdu literature from Pakistan. Let us talk about modernity in Urdu literature to try defining the concept in our own context, as distinct from the western model. A cursory examination sometimes reveals a strand of something imitative in some of our literatures. In fact, sometimes modernism here in the subcontinent seems like a deliberate imposition of abstraction on thought and expression. Do you think a native or an indigenous concept of modernism ever evolved in Urdu literature? How did western modernism as reflected in the writings of Proust, Eliot, and Joyce influence or take root in this soil? Do you think some features of modernism were simply superimposed on our literary traditions?

WAZIR AGHA: I'd first like to examine whether there is at all any literary movement which could be identified as 'modernism' here. Art in every age is modern and yet ancient, as ancient in value as the origin of man. The environment and mannerisms of the age in which a work of literature is produced are the natural components of the product. Any literary work worth its name is totally related to its time. That is what lends authenticity to the human experience being presented. And yet, inevitably, all good art is timeless.

Shakespeare is perhaps more alive in the twentieth century than in the sixteenth. The element of mystery in the phenomenon has still not been fully explained and the thesis has to be followed by an antithesis. What then is the relevance of being 'modern'? I think, basically, it has to be seen as a kind of confrontation of new ideas with the established old ones.

What happened at the time of Renaissance in the west a few centuries ago? The established concepts had become strictures and the unlimited imaginative and creative faculties of the human mind were being crushed. There was a need for fresh ideas to spread, noticeably and fast. A very interesting study I came across recently, Samuel Huntington's; he relates sudden surges of creative activity in the arts in history with climatic conditions! For instance he has statistics to prove that the Renaissance in Europe was simultaneous with an unusual number of thunder-storms!

Coming to the renaissance of ideas of the twentieth century, man suddenly felt uprooted from the security of the established metaphysics of human existence. Darwin with his *Evolution of Man*, Nietzsche, Kafka, Camus - the modern thinkers revolutionized the old thought patterns of the early twentieth century and made room for explorations of new ideas. Innovation, freedom, and creativity became new slogans. This was bound to affect the whole world.

S: Through experimentation and tremendous creative activity newer literary forms and thought processes are forever being created, but do you accept the idea of 'progress' in literature? Would you say that as people get more and more 'sophisticated', 'civilized', and technology-conscious there is a corresponding enhancement of general awareness in people about life and existence, which is demonstrated in literature too? Is today's literature more 'refined'?

WA: Language has to change with sensibility. When there is an intrinsic consciousness of the fragmentation of the world, of society and in fact of the human psyche, this inevitably projects itself in literature, in the kind of forms that could be expressive of such a phenomenon. Thus the need for new forms. The new world offers new experiences which in turn seek expression in the creative use of language. The macrocosm and microcosm are re-adjusted.

Spencer and Darwin in the nineteenth century shocked man into a realization that there was an animal hiding in every human being. This animal had to be unbridled and examined.

Religion had always attempted to suppress him. Also, there was a new concept of the 'superman' evolving through Nietzschean ideas. The emergence of Mussolini, Hitler, and the 007 hero created the perspective of the 'super' amongst humans and inspired yet again what one might call hero-worship. Where subjects so desire and there is a search for a torch-bearer, a leader emerges. Whether in mythology, religion, or in the history of thought, heroes were born when it was felt they were needed. The torch-bearers of the twentieth century, many of them products of the west, reached the Orient by virtue of the aggressive expansion of the west into the rest of the world.

S: Ironically, the heroes of philosophy, aesthetics, and various sciences inculcated an awareness of an individual as an 'anti-hero' - stressing the punitive nature and the essential insignificance of human existence in the vastness of the universe. What would you say about anti-heroes in modern fiction?

WA: I was talking about the negative aspect of hero-worship, mainly in political and ideological domains of society. In literature, the story has been different. The negation of the old ideas of the hero as an exceptionally powerful individual acquiring a central position in a novel or a poem was certainly set back in the twentieth century – there were too many heroes. What actually happened was, ordinary people started feeling and facing the challenge of cosmic mystery, made inescapable by the eruptions of the twentieth century – exactly as the heroes of the past had to confront it. So the 'anti-hero' is actually the everyday hero – the natural consequence and exemplar of heroes that emerged on a vast scale. In fact the political democratization of many countries helped to negate or at least drastically change the concept of the 'hero' and obviously of 'hero-worship' that went along with it.

S: In mid-twentieth century Hindi and Urdu fiction there's a noticeable - shall I say intrusion or emergence - of the 'outsider' as the hero. The central thematic concern of the writer seems to have been an exploration of this rather insular psyche with all its existential awareness. To what extent, I wonder, has this cross-pollination with western philosophical ideas been successful? I mean, does the 'oriental' ethos offer suitable ground for a healthy yield, or does the exercise yield merely a short-lived blossom for decorative vases in the drawing rooms of the sophisticated intellectuals of our countries?

WA: The world is smaller today. Cross-plantation or cross-fertilization of ideas between east and west has become an extremely common phenomenon, thanks to the media, satellite connections, etc... An awareness of alienation, I would say, is not the monopoly of the west. In this 'throw-away culture' when one can so easily throw away one's child or wife or husband, families are fast breaking up. Loneliness, an awareness of being alienated, and the birth of the outsider are but natural. Certainly, some amount of sifting of good literary expressions from bad would help identify the indigenous mode of delineation.

S: Modern literature emphasizes the 'transitory nature' of the self, questioning the stability of a total self resting on certainties found in religion and philosophy. Serious speculation on the 'nature of being' resulted in the fragmentation of the human psyche, of society, even of the dominant worldview. The traumatic experience of the two world wars created 'lost generations' and a hypersensitivity to the idea of death and the transitoriness of human existence.

WA: That's true but I'd like to bring your attention to a very crucial point as regards the literature of our own countries. There is a very clear distinction between the urban and rural mode of living and thinking in our own societies. While people in the villages may represent an integrated society even today, in the cities we have a different story to tell. Urban literature is, therefore, more akin to modern western literature. The experience of alienation is a major thematic concern of our urban writers, while our rural literature is essentially concerned with folklore and community life. The loneliness of a rural person is very different. It comes out of a different context.

S: Let us look at criticism in Urdu, in Pakistan, and in India. I think there is an inadequacy of serious and honest evaluation of Urdu literature. We have a very small body of theoretical critical work.

There hardly seems to be any tradition in criticism to strengthen or inspire critical responses in the common reader. Partisan approaches, conservatism, and a conspicuous lack of authentic critical reviewing of new literary work - all this is rather alarming. What do you think?

WA: In Pakistan, just as a lot of genuine creative writing is being done, a lot of critical work is being done as well. Excellent critical journals flourish through the extremely encouraging patronage of readers, as well as of professional critics and writers. But yes, there is indeed a glaring vacuum in the domain of criticism in Indian Urdu literature.

Political factionalism and vested interests of critics are factors contributing heavily to the erosion of a direct concern for the fact of literature. Every country has its own contexts - political, economic, and social. While an exposure to the outside is welcome, the critical approach must grow from its own roots. We tend to borrow a lot of western critical theory.

S: A healthy confrontation of ideas should produce not only a fertile atmosphere for critical thinking but also help the creative mind give birth to fresh resolutions, perhaps to old problems. Every age demands a re-adjustment of perspective.

WA: Yes, and this re-adjustment can take place through an upright and courageous confrontation with the 'movement' which is 'now'. That is what modernity is all about. Not the make-believe world of the future, not removed from present reality through a reliving of the obsolete past. The awareness of 'now' contains in itself a sense of the past and foresight, into the future, but it is like a tree with its roots in the present. And the development or rise into the sky is unrestrained and un-tabooed. That essential freedom to grow through the flux of time and space is vital for the total experience of the moment. My realization of the moment would be shaded with my being Pakistani and yours with your Indian-ness. A contact with modernity is established in creative writing when the words are charged with the power of offering real experience directly out of life to the reader.

S: I'd add that the role of the critic is to assess whether a piece of writing is literature or merely social documentation, propaganda, advice, or scholarly research. Only then should the literary work be evaluated for what we term literary merit.

WA: There is no doubt some stories are better than others and some are merely tales rather than stories. The critic should be able to identify whether the 'moment' in the story has been captured or not. This moment grows from its surroundings and finds symbolic expression in art. Each new work of art necessarily presents mythical thought-patterns and a fresh gush of strength to face reality... the experience of surrendering one's self to the moment. The moment in turn offers a certain kind of illumination. The writer keeps trying to relate himself to his reality, forever - to the reality of his past and future as well as his environs. In Alvin and Heidi Toffler's book *Future Shock* the present becomes a take-off point for the future. A total absorption or assimilation of the present creates the vision of the future which is actually experienced in the 'now'.

S: Post-modernist fiction in the west, particularly American fiction, demonstrates a coming together of journalism, reportage, and the conventional fictional form. Kurt Vonnegut, Doctorow, and some other American writers in this age of mass communication have popularized this new form. How about Pakistani Urdu writers? Are they also producing this form of creative communication?

WA: In the west there is a great deal of experimentation in every field - post-modern literature's slogan is 'innovation'. It is not the same in India and Pakistan. And of course, we do easily receive and accept some of the successful new forms here. We do have instances of effective usage of reportage in short fiction in Urdu.

S: How do you compare the Indian and Pakistani writers?

WA: One clear feature that comes to me easily is that while Pakistan has given birth to a greater number of poets in Urdu, in India there are more fiction writers. People somehow seem to be much more related to mundane reality there ... more of observation, a detailed survey of one's surroundings and weighing the odds and evens of a situation - all this I feel leads more to fiction and less to poetry which is much more abstract. I think it also has to do with Hindu society which indulges much less in abstract imaginative flights than perhaps Muslim society does.

S: The long history of foreign intrusion into India and the consequent exposure of Indians to diverse cultural impacts has lent, I think, a certain amount of flexibility and absorption of a variety of ideas.

WA: What I meant to say was that Hindu society is more embedded in soil and therefore closely related to social institutes whereas Muslim society has experienced wanderings, in parochial life as well as in the field of imagination. Hence its preoccupation with poetry. Actually whatever the art form, the artist seeks to examine the uniqueness of her experience in her art - her own particular psyche, cultural roots, nationality, and geographical position.

S: I'd add the experience the writer expresses has to be

her own - it has to be experienced first of all by herself. If it is borrowed, it'd only become an unnecessary burden on words that she may produce; the sagging words cannot then present even the semblance of art. May I ask you to name some writers you'd regard as leading Urdu short fiction?

WA: I am greatly moved by a number of living short fiction writers both from India and Pakistan - writers who have the potential to make history in literature and writers who are as worthy of attention as any great writer from anywhere in the world - Intizar Husain, Joginder Paul, Ghulam-ul-Saqlain Naqvi, Rashid Amjad, ManshaYad, Farkhanda Lodhi, among others.

S: Thank you so much for an insightful discussion.

Kathleen Raine

On Modernism and the Creative Process

KATHLEEN RAINE

KATHLEEN RAINE (1908-2003) was an exceptional poet and scholar who contributed significantly to the appreciation of spiritual traditions in British modernism. Her work included thirteen volumes of poetry, several books on William Blake, W. B. Yeats, and on the craft of poetry. She wrote a four-volume autobiography that concluded with India Seen Afar (1990). In 1980 she helped launch the well-known journal Temenos, and then continued for decades to edit this review devoted to 'the arts of the imagination'. The Temenos Academy instituted in 1990, made a persistent and concerted effort to bring about a re-appraisal and "reversal of the impoverished, reductionist view of humanity" that characterized Thatcher's England and the latter half of the twentieth century, as materialistic, nihilist, and relentlessly formalist. Kathleen Raine visited India in the late eighties as a guest of the Yeats Society for a seminar on "The Common Design". The following dialogue was inspired by her enthusiastic involvement in the seminar discussions on the modern temper and its reflection in literature.

SUKRITA: As students and teachers of modern English literature, we are well- attuned to experiments in literary forms. We revel in the idea of 'change' and the 'new' in literature, but what bothers me is that 'modernism' has now got to be almost totally identified with the notion of the 'new'. As a result, newness in form and content seems to have been accepted as a value in itself. Could you comment on the constraints this approach might prescribe for the writer? What about its negotiation with the enduring value of creative literature? How do you think the "modernist movement" and perhaps a writer like Yeats who was so rooted in 'tradition' responded to it?

KATHLEEN RAINE: Yeats' poetry was rooted in conventional metrics. He did not care to learn about free verse, as T. S. Eliot did. For Yeats – it was not as if he wanted to be 'conventional' or 'new'. Creative expression was something deeper for him. Music, of course, he felt was appropriate for the expression of the soul. What is rhythmic also has to be related to the 'essential'. What comes from the outer world has no rhythm. When that contact with the deeper self is lost, only then does the form break down. The link with the Centre demonstrates itself through rhythm in form. You see this breakdown of form, say, in cubist art, or in free verse, and it becomes an expression of alienation... Eliot's earlier poems are poems of tragic alienation. He had lost something and his poetry is the poetry of loss. After Eliot, the broken forms were retained without that sense of tragic loss. It became formulaic, merely a way of writing. For Eliot this break up of form had a lot of meaning. He was concerned with loss of contact with the Centre. In Yeats' words, "the centre cannot hold". Moreover, Eliot was aware that his poetry was the poetry of alienation. Later, free verse became popular because everybody thought it very easy to write since there were no formal rules to follow. Yeats never wrote free verse at all. And I think those who write from their imaginative Centre rather than writing about its loss will necessarily have some sense of concrete form and rhythm. Those who are not concerned with the essential link between Centre and deeper self cannot generate art – by merely imitating. You *can* produce metric verse by imitation. For example, the eighteenth century did produce a whole lot of verse structures. But this type of versification was acquired and learnt. Forms proper, for the poetry of the imaginative Centre, cannot be learnt; they have to be generated from within.

S: Yes, if form is superimposed on experience the expression would be too contrived and prohibitive for a spontaneous involvement of the reader. In order to be able to retain the freshness of the creative experience in literary expression, it may be essential for a writer to have some measure of freedom and licence to operate effectively.

KR: Herbert Read quotes Coleridge and says "form is proceeding and shapes superimposed". Form, in reality, proceeds from life itself, as in the form of a plant. It grows from life itself. You can only make an artificial rose by imitating ... a rose without fragrance.

S: The seminar in Delhi that you recently attended, on 'the common design' of creative expression across diverse arts and cultural conditioning patterns, generated impassioned scholarly discussions, specially on the east-west binary. How would you view modern Indian writing in this context?

KR: I am much less familiar with Indian writing than I'd wish to be. One reason of course is that I can only read writers who write in English, those who may be arguably already alienated from their Indian-ness. Some of whom seem to imitate what they perceive as the west. This does not help. We look for the Voice of India. 'Somehow you have to locate the right idiom and the right language. Tagore made the right choice by writing in his tongue, Bengali. Yeats would have made a similar choice. But then I can see the problem, the problem for someone like yourself who is in a difficult predicament, of not having a similar choice. What is your language? In what language will your soul speak? It is indeed a complex predicament. Perhaps the Indian writer in English has learnt to speak for herself in the English language too. It is important to sift the good from the bad and for that critical tools need to be developed. Some of the Indian novelists, for instance R.K. Narayan and Kamala Markandaya in her *Nectar in a Sieve* (1954) have of course successfully communicated themselves and India to us.

S: It is interesting to see how while the 'east-west encounter', to use a critical cliché, is being conceptualised more realistically today, the common currents between the east and the west too are being worked out. There is a tremendous cross-cultural interflow… imperialist and otherwise.

KR: What actually happens is that a lot many times the west dominates and imposes itself on the east. What I find, for instance in the Indian universities, is scholars having undergone a complete process of westernization, thanks to the British system of education initiated in the colonial times. The same ideas, the same approach! In fact, many Indian universities are at times more British than the universities in Britain. The cultural imperialism of the west has entirely seeped through. It's not just the question of the east or the west; it is to do with two contrary ideologies, two different views of life. What we call 'west' is generally perceived as a materialistic view of man. We weren't always that. After all, even upto the Romantics, there was a spiritual view of man. But increasingly materialism has imposed itself, not only in our technology, which we obviously need, but also in our ideology.

Man is now looked upon as a mechanism. Inevitably, sooner or later, man is devalued in terms of meaning and value.

He becomes a part of a meaningless universe. Whatever he does loses meaning and dignity. There's reduction in the image of man, a reductionism that ultimately leads to nihilism, and that seems to me the point we have just about reached. People in England talk about Francis Bacon as the greatest painter. An able painter no doubt, but, what is he painting? He is painting a screaming corpse! And according to his philosophy that is what man is... a screaming corpse which can keep itself animated only by injecting himself with violence and despair. He despairs, of course.

S: This sensitive awareness of what a human being becomes or is reduced to should create a consciousness of the need to look back and search for the original, the elemental man, you mean? Does the artist, in one sense, shake up the complacent acceptance of the new and sensational philosophical theories about what a human being is?

KR: I hope so! We began *Temenos*, you know, to reaffirm what is being lost, and to point out that the currently prevalent view of man is false.

S: Perhaps, to make doubt and suspicion a religion will only encourage perversities.

KR: Well, nihilism has already become a matter of faith. Even poets like Sylvia Plath. Suicide and death were the two terrible obsessions of that poet. She was in reality a victim of her society. The American society, I think, has to bear the responsibility for her neurosis. An intelligent, sensitive young woman has nothing to nourish her soul within that kind of society.

S: But then, wasn't Plath herself enamoured of a poet such as Yeats. In *The Bell Jar*, which is more or less her own life story, she describes how she went looking for a house to rent and was thrilled to get Yeats'. Once inside she roamed around charged with an elated feeling of occupying the house of a great poet. She waited for the moment of inspiration which could produce poetry of Yeats' genius. But when she does write poetry it is completely different, somewhat an expression of the fragmentation of herself, quite contradictory to Yeats' very vision of existence. How do you perceive this feature?

KR: Well, what is art for? If you say that art is merely the mirror in which society can be read or is reflected, then the daily newspaper is enough. That too is a medium through which the voice of society is articulated. But then art is different. It is the language of the spirit, of a certain inspiration which is filtered through the individual. Every artist discovers his own form and style to express the uniqueness of his spirit, his own culture. Materialistic philosophy recognizes only one level, the material.

It does not take cognizance of any higher level of existence. There is a hierarchy of disposition ... the body, the soul or spirit and then the Source. If the higher levels are denied recognition in art, then the product can only have ephemeral value. As I.A. Richards rightly pointed out, "poetry is the house of the soul." Yeats called it the city of Byzantium. Fine arts build for the human soul its environment. We don't merely live within material walls. We live amidst the totality of a culture that is rooted in a spiritual vision which has a spiritual source. Yeats saw this very clearly. He said, listen to the falconer… "the falcon cannot hear the falconer" so "the centre cannot hold". Yeats came like the falconer. In every age there are one or more voices trying to renew man's contact with the Source. Eliot lamented its loss and tried to get it back. He was a very fine poet. But Yeats' poetry is positive; his poetry has in it all that poetry should have, a total vision of man. He started from the ground, the land of Ireland, its history, its people. But his poetry takes its life from the eternal spring. The Source is always there.

S: And one type of Modernism, an aggressively overpowering movement, demonstrated a complete break with anything spiritual ...glorifying the 'primitive' by making an ostensibly 'rational' theoretical place for the 'irrational man'. So, either man was viewed as a mechanized robot or as though living merely by instinct like an animal.

KR: Yet, it isn't as if the modern man is living in a different world. It's just that he has cut himself off through ideology. It is not a matter of east and west; it is one ideology against the other. The materialist view of the universe may have enabled scientific development but it has not enabled life. Someone like Sylvia Plath unknowingly denied her own inner life just perhaps to become different.

S: Can we trace Plath's predicament to sometting in to past a bit? The obsession with death and the urgency to make the most of each moment was an obvious characteristic of the 'lost generation'. Not being able to cope with new realities caused frustration and bitterness, and we see philosophers and artists grappling with what they view as the meaninglessness of life. Of course, later this was no longer a "felt experience". It became more and more fashionable to talk more about death than about life.

KR: Yes, Sylvia Plath was exposed to a materialistic ideology that has roots in the previous generation's experiences of the first World War. We started *Temenos* with the express purpose of combating a current, call it western. The secular materialist values which prevail all over the world had to be rebutted. Tradition, as Coomaraswamy calls it, is not of the past – it is contact with reality. It is present for all time. Each time it is a renewed contact with reality itself.

S: You are yourself an established poet; shall we now talk about the creative process, that is, the process of writing poetry?

KR: Yeats said that the divine genius is a kind of crisis

that synthesizes or unites the sleeping and the waking mind. There is an expansion of the consciousness, an extension into a wider field. I believe in inspiration because I believe in the Source. Inspiration can be more intense or a little less: you can wake up in that one moment and the day shines for you. All great poetry offers a tremendous opening up. You don't lose what you have. Your own specific knowledge is retained but everything synthesizes. It is the uniting of everything. Everything is brought into focus, everything that you know and are, and even something that's beyond you. All comes into focus and one's self keeps expanding and learning. It keeps taking in larger and larger experience, increasing in scope. For great poets, poetry is not a mere expression. They embrace a certain situation at a specific time and place. Poetry is a total statement of their culture and of their world. Today, poetry does not seem to do that. True poetry must take the responsibility for heeding its age.

S: It is interesting to see that the more specific you are the more related you are with the moment. And the more related and specific you are, the more universal your poetry is.

KR: Absolutely. There is no such thing as international poetry. You have to be related to that very petal of that very flower. That becomes the focus for the whole vision. Every individual is the centre of the whole universe, opening out her or his own time, place and situation while at the same time it goes beyond. So a poet like Tagore who is so regional becomes a world poet and his poetry speaks to the whole world. He was the focus for something particular in the universe. Yeats too was very clear about that. He is concerned only with the images of his own country. Each of us takes in the whole of heaven and earth and makes a prison for one's self.

S: Lack of relatedness inevitably results in a feeling of having gone astray. What do you think, is this a dominant characteristic of contemporary poetry?

KR: In reality, loss of faith has become a matter of faith.

S: Thank you Dr Raine for your words of inspiration and caution. We wish you and *Temenos* a long and energetic life, if only to save literature from the sheer morbidity of singing to death rather than celebrating life.

KR: Thank you.

Margaret Chatterjee

On the 'Modern' in Indian Literature

MARGARET CHATTERJEE

MARGARET CHATTERJEE taught philosophy at Delhi University, and served as Professor of Comparative Religion at Visva-Bharati, Shantiniketan. She was Visiting Professor at Drew University and later, she was Director, Indian Institute of Advanced Study, Shimla. President of the International Society for Metaphysics, and an editorial consultant for several journals, she edited Contemporary Indian Philosophy through 1974 and The Philosophy of Nikunja Vihari Banerjee in 1989. Her publications include several articles in academic and scholarly journals, five volumes of poetry, one volume of short stories and a series of books on different aspects of Indian philosophy, existentialism, Gandhi, and religious plurality. Chatterjee is also the author of Our Knowledge of Other Selves *(1963),* Gandhi's Jewish Friends *(1992),* Hinterlands and Horizons, Excursions in Search of Amity *(2002), and* Lifeworlds, Philosophy, and India Today *(2005). She is also well known as a music critic.*

SUKRITA: Perhaps we could begin with a discussion on the idea of modernity in the context of the artist's expression and creative consciousness. Each age expresses its own imaginative construct of reality through an expression of the individual's essential freedom.

At the outset I'd draw a distinction between modernity and modernism. Modern culture expresses itself in the implements of technological advancement, dynamism, physical and metaphysical migrations, and newness – not in an abstract sense but in the 'real'. 'Modernism' on the other hand, as reflected in the works of literary modernists such as Yeats, Eliot, Pound, or Proust celebrates a fixed and knowable past and opposes the trajectory of 20th century culture. The crises or the perception of reality as fragmented necessitated a reactive construct of modernism in the West. How do you understand this phenomenon, philosophically?

MARGARET CHATTERJEE: Let me just react to one thing you've said - that most poets reacted against technology. But then remember there is a line in one of Sitwell's poems "Jane, Jane/Tall as a crane. The morning light creaks down again." When that poem came out people were a little horrified by the word "creak", seeing it only as an onomatopoeic device. But then she used the metaphor "crane" for a tall person, which showed it wasn't the bird but the machine. So it isn't that people, poets or writers or artists always reacted against technology. We live in a technological civilization after all.

S: I was thinking of what the coming of technology did to the consciousness of writers like D.H. Lawrence, perhaps. And it sparke a curiosity, or rethinking, reflected in movements such as Primitivism. Nostalgia for the past, concern for tradition, the call for the 'elemental' moved protest

convincingly against change and novelty. Reactions to the

dehumanization that the machine culture may have brought are evidenced much later in the Indian context

M C: I find it difficult to generalize. For one thing I wouldn't put Yeats, Eliot, and Proust together. If you are talking about reactions to war in the early twentieth century - the poets of the Great War and immediately after, and poets of the forties and after, echoing them, I'd say they were all horrified by war rather than by technology as such.

S: The questioning, scepticism and a temper of crisis... the impact of war and mass displacement… All this is relevant too to post-Partition India.

MC: I think all kinds of strands came in. "the centre does not hold", as Yeats said. The frame is large and I wouldn't take that as a protest against technology per se, or alone. I think this is a multi-faceted thing which doesn't have only one aspect. In his book *The Sea of Faith* Don Cupitt takes up a famous line from Matthew Arnold where Arnold is describing the way the tide is retreating and carrying the pebbles with it and he speaks of the "retreating tides of faith." But the analysis of that wouldn't be Arnold's if we applied it to this century. So it is with warfare, the experience of wars. There are many wars, but post-War refers to a very specific one. In a way it is simply not part of the Indian psyche to the extent that it is part of the psyche of people from the continent or even from England and America. Even America is on the fringe. They came into the war late and it was not part of their experience of modernism. Their modernism seems to me yet again different. I look upon modernism as a very diverse phenomenon and I don't think one will get very far by trying to find a core which applies everywhere.

S: I am trying to work out how 'modernism' can be defined in the context of early twentieth-century Western literature, as well as how our own literature projects a modernistic stance, though perhaps a couple of decades later. As the ideas were assimilated and nativized, as it were, there seems to be a synthesis between the Indian writer's own sense of tradition and heritage and ideas from the West. Though one may say that, sociologically, the writer doesn't have first-hand cultural experience, short stories by writers like Kashinath Singh, Nirmal Verma, and others clearly demonstrate how some of those ideas have been convincingly contextualized here.

MC: You virtually conceded a rather interesting point - which seems to be that the Indian writer dealt with modern phenomena at second-hand because she or he was seeing it through the lens of a literature which is in fact not the literature of her native soil.

S: Well, though it may not be a native cultural phenomenon, modernism received from the West does undoubtedly undergo a process of indigenization and modification. I think we must acknowledge the role of leaders like Gandhi who helped India modernize with an eye on tradition.

MC: Nirad Chaudhuri's book *A Passage to England* is a very good example to be cited here. He analyses and shows how the Indian experience of the upper middle class - he's thinking mainly of Bengal but it probably applies everywhere - was filtered through the experience of English literature which enabled people to appropriate (I would use appropriate rather than imitate) a whole landscape as well as a set of values which go back to Greece and Rome. This brings up the question of Enlightenment values and I think some people in India wanted to be thought of as their guardians. You get the rather unfortunate term 'Bengal Renaissance' - unfortunate because if you compare the people who are usually put into that slot, Rabindranath Tagore and so on, you realise at once it has nothing to do with the Renaissance at all, because the Renaissance as a term in the Western history of ideas refers to the revival of classical learning. So what they were talking about was the Enlightenment and not really the Renaissance at all. And the reaction to the Enlightenment was many-faceted too. It was mainly a central European phenomenon, not an English phenomenon, and Nietzsche belonged to it with his discovery of the deep and dark - the Dionysian as opposed to the Apollonian. You can see that all this is very far removed from the 'Indian experience', 'Indian sensibility', but you are right that a lot of it has been appropriated. Often appropriated with an uneasy conscience. I think some people write about peasant life instead of writing about the middle class: they ease their conscience that way, by talking about their 'own' people.

S: Yes. Also the genuine writer's approach to the peasants or to his/her own people invariably changes after his sensibility has been exposed to ideas from outside. I have in mind somebody like PhanishwarRenu whose modern sensibility convincingly delineates the peasant. Was it his exposure to 'global ideas' that actually helped him arrive at his descriptions with freshness and originality?

MC: That's it! I would say the sensibility of the sensitive writer is perhaps seventy per cent cosmopolitan at least. And this is a universal phenomenon – it's true in any country, whether Latin American or Black, or whatever else. The cosmopolitan quality is built into what you might call being 'modern'. Whether it is itself modern or not in the sense *you* want to pin it down is another question. It mightn't be. You might be more concerned with another dimension.

S: When I refer to modernism, literary modernism, I understand it as a distinct wave, incoming and outgoing. 'Modernity 'to me refers to time in the linear sense – a progression. There is that significant suggestion of disconnection and loss of the past, while modernism seems to respond/react to the present. It would be interesting to think of the relationship between tradition and modernity, and then between tradition and modernism.

MC: Well, at the end of the nineteenth century the traditionalists were revivalists, not in any romantic sense but in a quite frankly reactionary political sense. And I think there is an enormous lobby still around, their numbers unfortunately on the increase, who will continue to talk of tradition because they want to put the clock back politically, socially and in every way, on fuzzy grounds of 'Indianness'. This is what I see around me, and it is connected with xenophobia and so on - all of which I find absolutely anti-modern.

S: What would you say then about Rudolph's analysis of what Gandhiji was trying to do? He talks about how Gandhi modernizes 'tradition' by using conventionally 'Indian' means, rooted in Indian culture. Say, through the use of satyagraha, maunvrata, ahimsa, to achieve ends which emphasise the dignity of the human being and her awareness of her rights. But the means that he employs are 'traditional'; there is a sort of revivalism in that.

MC: Definitely, yes!

S: But along with it, the process of modernization is taking place in a rather subtle way.

MC: If you look at Ernest Gellner's book *Thought and Change*, towards the end you find him acknowledging very clearly that this is going to break apart at the seams because you can't eat your cake and have it too, and, which is (forgive my saying so) what people are trying to do in India today. It just can't be done. A time will come when there'll be a realization that if you are going to have modern things you've got to have a completely different concept of time, which is governed by some of the things that people don't like, namely the factory rhythm of life, rushing off to work at six a. m., being quick, not being sloppy - none of which in fact belong to the 'Indian ethos' as the mainstream frames it. Some of these things Gandhiji did try to bring in. But we can also see that it's been washed away by the seas of time, nothing has been left. It has, perhaps, got to do with the nature of the majority of Hindu society, its ability to assimilate and its ability to destroy. You do have a veneer of modernization, but inside I think there's very little that's modern.

S: Would you say that there are two streams or various levels at which it is functioning? Is there any synthesis at all that you see between the 'Indian' and the 'modern'?

MC: I think since Independence some kind of effort has been made by some people to synthesize, but it's very obviously not working. I think one just has to look around, to see a pretty dismal record, and that record can be analysed and diagnosed. I'm not a Marxist but if we can read the signs, all around us we can see a return to some of the most backward and the most revivalist forms of society and thinking there have ever been in India. I'm sorry to say this. I think a very tiny percentage of people are modern at all. Being capable of producing certain sorts of technology is one phenomenon, and people in fact buying it and using it - that is something else.

S: Many Latin American writers, particularly Garcia Marques, project a sort of hallucinatory realism in their fiction. *A Hundred Years of Solitude*, they say, is 'magical realism'. Would you say that such a stance and style are closer to the Indian rather than the modern Western approach, which is preoccupied with the avant-garde, with novelty and the like?

MC: I don't know! Unless by that you mean the piling on of details which don't make sense? In a way that's what we see around us - a multitude of details which in fact do not make sense.

S: No, I've a different context in mind. Reference for instance to the 'other world', dialogues with the dead, and the dead seeming to exist along with the living. It's not superstition, but it's kind of a realization or sensitivity to the world beyond, an acceptance of that world, a kind of sense of the occult.

MC: It's closer to the African way of looking at things

than to the Indian at the moment.

S: It is indeed very difficult to generalize in India since there is so much diversity - one doesn't see any distinct movement. That is why criticism in Hindi and Urdu doesn't talk of movements, it speaks of decades - the short-story of the fifties, of the sixties. Each writer seems to be carrying her own distinct kind of reality, in her own style and through her own methods of expression.

MC: Yes! That's rather good, isn't it? I mean the discovery of individuality has to come first.

S: And that also reflects on the kind of society this is – unequivocally diverse.

MC: But doesn't the path-breaking writer always stand apart from society in some way or the other?

S: Well, when it comes to English literature it seems much easier to locate three or four significant writers who have a similar approach. I don't know if it has something to do with the critical perception here, in Hindi and Urdu. Although there's no dearth of creative literature of course, there isn't any sense of 'schools' of criticism that critics have managed to evolve in the modern period.

MC: How can there be? Are we comparing centuries of English criticism with, say, eighty years of literature in the vernacular languages here? The time span is quite different.

S: Not exactly. I am trying to collate eighty years of English criticism and eighty years of criticism in the vernaculars... Neither seems to impress. While creative concerns do appear to be similar, here and in the West, critical approaches have not been evolved in India in the modern period.

MC: Well, perhaps because creative critical thinking is not encouraged in academia. It is the literate and elitist class which is writing for the most part. If you ever have a situation where you have got your genuine peasant writer who is catapulted straight from a primary school and is able to write well, that would be a new literature and that would indeed be something. Writers have by and large come from the privileged classes - privileged vis-a-vis the rest of the country.

S: In contexts that are specifically Indian, some modern Hindi and Urdu short stories clearly demonstrate a change, say, in interpersonal relationships, the approach to women, and in the expression of the individual self. Rajinder Singh Bedi's novel *Ek Chadar Maili Si* is the projection of an Indian situation with a 'progressive' perspective.

MC: Let me give you one more literary example. I'll mention Nirad Chaudhuri again. He has a book in Bengali about women characters. He has a theory, which is being discussed quite a bit among Bengali litterateurs, about the role of Bankim Chandra's novels on the writing of the novel. His theory is that in terms of theme and treatment, the concept of passion enters into Bengali stories thanks to Bankim having brought that element into his novels. This is in fact an alien concept in Indian literature compared to passion as understood by, say, Zola or some of the other Continental novelists. Now today, Bengali novels have as much to do with the bedroom as any western novel. The system of arranged marriages, the rigid caste system - all this in a sense closes the door to the expression of any form of tenderness. This is noticeable by all visitors from abroad - the lack of tenderness in Indian life. Now if this is true, there's bound to be a crippling of the sensibility, right at the grass-roots. You have writers in the West writing about female frigidity in India. There may be a certain lacuna in Indian literature - certain things which are not treated for the simple reason that people don't feel like that, behave like that. Unless you do have a dimension of tenderness, it'd indeed be difficult to have wholesome literature. The story, it seems to me, has gone by the wayside - the plot, the characters.

S: Well, if you mean the narrative in the conventional sense, yes, that may be so. But certainly in the new story, a pattern does evolve, in its own style, though there may not be the linear, sequential narration of events or a chronology being maintained. The concern is with a different consciousness', the moment explored creatively through a character or a situation where things connect.

MC: .... connect and then fall apart again! This is why, frankly, a great deal of contemporary literature is unreadable. Much more effort on the part of the reader is required now. People are not intrinsically interested in the experience described. There's nothing to learn or be entertained by. That's why people like George Steiner are saying over and over again that maybe literature is on its way out. Any writer now has to compete also with visual media.

S: I think of writers such as Beckett who are striving, through words, to reach what's called 'Literature of Silence'. In his TV film *Not I* the camera is focussed on a dumb woman who has suddenly found speech. There's a close-up of the grotesque horror, of the desperate movements of the mouth, the sticky tongue, the lips and so forth, caught in the process of speaking in a gush because there's a danger of her losing speech again; Beckett's concern with speech, the cacophony of words, finds another expression in this play.

MC: Certainly, "time is being cut out and silence screams". It's there in Brecht, in Sartre - a rather catastrophic situation. But, another thing - and this is something to be sad about - these days the writer on the whole is writing for other writers, not for the public at all. Anyway, in a country where there are masses of illiterate people a very small number is going to read them.

S: What do you have to say about 'newer' forms of writing for newer sensibilities? And how would the concept of 'progress' in literature fit in?

MC: The concept of progress is under fire anyway. If you ask me, has there been progress in literature, I'd say no, but that's probably because I am old fashioned enough to think the element of enjoyment to be got from 'modern' literature is nil. The basic question is whom one is writing for. Each speaks in her own voice. But very often it's the language of the other.

S: Well, many concepts and theories worked out by philosophers and psychologists seem to originate in earlier creative literary contexts...

MC: That is what is said about Aristotle, that logic after all existed before Aristotle chose to write about it; grammar existed before the grammarians put it down on paper. I don't see any 'progress'.

S: But then, changing sensibilities do require fresh adjustments. When there is a change in the experience of reality and newer perceptions are available, the mode of creative expression does also change.

MC: As I said, the basic question is whom one is writing for. Only Hindi speaking readers will read literature in Hindi unless it is lucky enough to have translators. There are small regional literatures, and there is literature in world languages.

S: The problem of the accessibility of literatures from regional languages is certainly real, but I'd say it is more a problem for the curious reader than for the writer herself.

MC: Well each person, as I said, speaks in her own voice. The problem often arises when one speaks in someone else's voice. But that too is inevitable. There are influences. There are people who move from place to place... take a Sindhi for example - she's living in Bombay and writing. Now, she can't invoke the old Sindh anymore and if she's born after the partition she hasn't been there or even seen that culture. The language she's carrying does not have the original echoes and overtones.

S: The writer in such a case seeks a new idiom, a new language perhaps, to express her changed reality.

MC: Probably what people do then is to write in their own

language and also write in the world language to reach a wider public.

S: Such a feature perhaps would create peculiar tensions in the creative activity of the writer.

MC: There's bound to be a to-ing and fro-ing unless one is a black writer in America. Even there you are carrying a sort of cultural load which is no longer alive to you. You've never been to Africa, you don't know the language, and yet you are aware of something ancestral. As far as India is concerned, you are right, there's a sort of cultural baggage which is carried anyway. And, if carried cheerfully and with a sense of richness, there is less of a split personality. And in a society such as that of India, where there are problems of survival, 'unreal' questions such as that of 'alienation' are inapplicable. They are 'imported' ideas, not experiences.

S: Where and how does the 'global consciousness' of the modern writer adjust itself to the specific cultural context has indeed to be examined very sensitively and delicately for a proper appreciation of modern literature. Thanks indeed for sounding this alert, and for being so candid in your expression!

M.M. Agrawal

On the Ascent of Modernity in India

M.M. Agrawal

M.M. Agrawal was a Fellow of the Indian Institute of Advanced Study, Shimla, and read Philosophy at Birkbeck College, University of London. Subsequently, he taught for nearly twenty years at various universities in Egypt and Nigeria. In teaching and writing, his central concern was the understanding and re-evaluation of world spiritual philosophy in light of contemporary systems of thought to construct a holistic picture of human life. Among his many publications, The Philosophy of Non-Attachment *(1983) is an outstanding example of his contribution to the study of Indian philosophy.*

SUKRITA: As an Indian philosopher with first-hand experience of western scholarship, culture, and ethos, you are perhaps appropriately placed to comment on the philosophic and literary milieu of post-Independence Indian society. What do you think freedom has brought us? How do you compare the pre-Independence temper with the post-? Did something significant happen to the Indian psyche after it acquired political freedom as a consequence of long struggle?

M.M. Agrawal: I'd say that in post-Independence India nothing completely new emerged. When I say 'new', I am thinking of value systems, of philosophy, ethics and values in general. But a lot of new things came into being in the beginning of the present century. That was the period when our society was undergoing really radical change. We don't realize it because we think only of our people fighting for political independence. But there was a whole cultural revolution, an axiological revolution, going on at that time. This came about, I think, largely under the leadership of Mahatma Gandhi once he arrived on the Indian scene in the1920's. So in order to understand the new India, one has to look at that period of modern Indian history very carefully - the period of about forty or fifty years before Independence, the period which is generally referred to as the Indian Renaissance. Perhaps it'd be better to call this a period of both Renaissance as well as Enlightenment.

What happened in this period was that a lot of new values which were 'imported' into the country through British influence and had been operating on the intellectual level, limited to the elite, were made to work in social and political fields - not so much in the economic field because we were not yet free to handle our economy ourselves. The social structure began to change while we were still under British rule. These values, I'd say, were secular in their ends in the broadest sense. For the first time we really recognized what it means to have human dignity in a social context, what it means to have justice, equality, and collective responsibility for the development of every individual. It's then that modernity dawned upon us and it was in this age that secular ideas, rational thought, and the scientific outlook came into play. People now actually wanted these values to be realized in social activity. These aspirations were to be realized through the political movement itself. I call this modernity.

The term 'modern' in the broadest sense of the word refers to the 'present' period of any time. Today is modern relative to yesterday. Human life is never static. Civilization is in the process of perpetual flux. Relative to the past, any time therefore is modern. But, from time to time we find, it just so happens that a completely new outlook towards life emerges, bringing with it a completely new set of values which apply to life as a whole. This happens when human knowledge makes a significant leap into the unknown. There is a significant and rapid broadening of the horizon of human understanding.

S: But do you think this actually happened in the Indian context? It certainly did in the West. Indeed there were Indians who brought new ideas from the west, but this was very much on the periphery. The changing Indian consciousness seems to emerge in literature not in the early twentieth century but much later, after Independence, in the late 50's or so. It is then that modernity seems to dawn here in the way that it did in the early-twentieth-century western world.

MMA: Yes, I entirely agree with you, as far as literature is concerned. Literature tends to reflect the structure and the processes of society when they've already crystallized. The struggle for social change is inevitably precursor to the change evident in literature. That is why I said, in order to understand the post-Independence age even in literature, one has to look back at pre-Independence society. Modernity may not have shown up in literature then but in other spheres of life it certainly made its appearance. After all most of India was illiterate and our primary aim at the time was political freedom. What mattered then was direct action backed by social and religious philosophy. Vivekananda, Gandhi, Brahmo Samaj, Arya Samaj and others were engaged in action in one or the other way through political, religious or philosophical thought. I call *this* modernity. All those new values brought with them new aims and purposes. Our fundamental aim of course was to attain freedom, which implied a total reorganization of our lives and society. In this you see western influence in its most concrete form. We didn't think in these terms earlier.

S: How would you define the relationship between tradition and modernity conceptually? In India modernity did not come as the kind of revolution the west saw. There has been a gradual assimilation of certain values, along with a negotiation with western ideas. The philosophical sorting began much later. It took a long time even for Gandhi to have an impact – for a suitable intervention in the evolution of ideas and values. Perhaps because our society *is* characteristically traditionalist, modernity took a long time to become an operational concept.

MMA: Modernity was not a revolution but its impact does begin to show itself in the early twentieth century. That's why I'd like to call the period both a Renaissance and Enlightenment. This will be clearer if we understand the relationship between modernity and tradition. I'd like to draw parallels here with the relationship between revolution and tradition or revolution and history, of the old with the new, of the past with the present, etc. Many people tend to think that a 'revolution' is a complete rejection of the past but this is not so. A revolution necessarily requires a past. A better word than rejection perhaps is 'surpassing' - the surpassing of the past, to use a Sartrean term, in the present, to create something new; but there *is* something to surpass or put aside. So the now is always related to the past. Although revolution may imply rejection, there is no total rupture with the past. The same applies to the relation between modernity and tradition. In order for the new to be accepted there has to be a moral authority justifying the change, and a relevant present as something to be accepted.

S: But from where would this moral authority emerge?

MMA: It can only come from its own axiological resources, from its own past. In the past, therefore, there are both – the elements that have to be surpassed and elements that are going to bestow upon the new a justification, by way of providing moral authority. I'd say then that modernity has a love-hate relationship with tradition. It draws its justification from the very past it seems to be rejecting.

When it comes to the Indian scene, the new values that appeared in the beginning of this century were scientific, rational, and secular in character and these values were a bit different from the established ones at the time. The few who were familiar with them were perhaps aware of modern changes. For the contemporary majority these values were alien but the aim was invariably to make them work in their own sphere of life, particularly in the political and social spheres.

S: But then there'd be a need for a cultural revolution. I wonder if that ever took place here.

MMA: I think it did. But it was not shouted out as cultural revolution. I think it was presented in the cloak of self actualization as society, under the aegis of the freedom movement. Look at the work of Mahatma Gandhi, and of others who may not have been so directly involved in politics, such as Vivekananda who propounded a social interpretation of religion and emphasized ethics much more than worship and ritual. This, I think, is an element of cultural revolution. Gandhi, as is well-known, rejected the inheritance of such ugly practices as the caste system, Zamindari, and other social discrimination.

S: But these names can be counted on finger-tips, as it were. And even today, many decades after Mahatma Gandhi, we still have the same problems at the very grass-roots of our society. The ideas that were floating around then perhaps did not effectively or functionally reach the majority.

MMA: Well, I don't think there's been *in*significant change in Indian society. Maybe one cannot call it a revolution per se because it's not been sudden, abrupt, or whole-sale, but it's been slow and continuous. The process of change was initiated then and has by now achieved a great deal. Because it's hidden and slow and continuous, we don't often recognize how much Indian society has changed culturally in terms of social values in the last fifty years or so, from the time of Gandhi. One has to recall how things were half a century ago, the constrictive social institutions we had, restricted human relationships, orthodoxy, and so on, to be able to appreciate the changes in this society. Undoubtedly the process has been gradual. I don't believe any cultural change can come suddenly, in a revolutionary way, though the attempt does damage. There are examples, China and some other countries, that tried and failed. A cultural or social revolution which implies a change of values and outlook is always a slow and continuous process. What's also important to understand is how this change took place on Indian soil when the some of the ideas we are referring to were alien. The link between the old and the new had to be established. The justification of the new had to come from the old itself - from tradition. Again, Gandhi is a very good example. The sophisticated, legal, and secular ideas, actually the whole conception of political structure, were presented by Gandhi by reinterpreting our spiritual and religious past. He connected progressive and modern values with a source in the past, in our spiritual philosophy. So by drawing upon the reserves of spiritual and philosophical heritage he provided a moral justification for the adoption of those values which on the face of it were alien and new to our contemporaneous culture.

S: Perhaps it would be interesting to see how one could distinguish between imitative lifestyles and lifestyles adopted through assimilation of attitudes and ideas from outside. Even in literature what we need to sift is the authentic from the imitative.

MMA: In any modernity, customary authority not moral authority, is rejected. Some version of moral authority is used to justify the rejection and the adoption of new values. In India moral authority was gathered from within a part of Indian culture itself. Thus the process of accepting new values cannot be thought about as mere imitation. To take to new ideas and values when the process is backed with a consciousness that relates to our own past is indeed going to trigger a process of 'owning' those values.

S: How does Gandhi help provide moral authority? How does he relate the new with the past?

MMA: Let me give you an example: when Gandhi attacks the social structure or the caste system and when he makes the untouchables 'Harijans', he appeals to the same Vedas, the same spiritual literature from which these distinctions are drawn. He'd quote from the Gita that God resides in the heart of everyone and so everyone is equal. He'd refer to our spiritual literature and the ethics seemingly inherent to it, to fight against injustices prevailing in society. So he could take these secular values and receive them via familiar classical ancient values and relate them to our lives. That's how he tried to convince people that these values are to be accepted.

A literary form cannot flourish without reference to the realities of social and societal life. Secondly, its novelty is its axiological justification, especially where it is used, regardless of whether it may historically speaking have originated elsewhere. I think both the above criteria are satisfied in the case of the Indian situation.

S: I would now like to refer to the literary and aesthetic movement we call 'modernism', one version of which involves a celebration of a fixed knowable past in the western context. Eliot, Joyce, and others consciously celebrated the past and advocated a strong sense of tradition. In our arts and culture when literary modernism appears in the 50's and 60's, our traditionalist society presents very little resistance to newness sans tribute to tradition... One doesn't see the same lament for lost values here as in the west, does one?

MMA: The explanation for this actually lies in what I said earlier. In England there's a greater rupture with the past. The arrival of modern science and technology created a kind of upheaval and a society in which values of interpersonal relationships and the classical virtues were difficult to uphold. A lot of writers and artists reacted and wanted to go back to the past. Actually, what I see as central to European modernism is the impact of the concept of human freedom. The central feature of modernity is the realization that man is absolutely free, not only to choose from amongst the given values but also to create new ones. This consciousness came to Europe in the earlier century due to work done by people like Darwin, Freud, Einstein, Marx, etc. I think the confrontation with one's freedom became a bit difficult to cope with. Well, it became unbearable - and you find this expressed in philosophy. Sartre says, one tries to conceal one's freedom from oneself because with freedom comes the responsibility of constructing one's being through one's own choices. There are then no essential values which ought to determine our behaviour. Many people reacted to that outlook. Those writers who had a nostalgia for the past, I'd say, looked backwards not so much because of the horrors of new civilization but because they couldn't cope with newfound freedom. New science, technology, and society have given a sense of new power to man. I should think wisdom lies in learning to harness this power, which can change man's destiny and can be an asset. Of course, some did face up to it. There are two types of writers, those who reacted and couldn't cope with this freedom, and those who could; they did create new forms to match the new sensibility.

S: In the west the process of philosophically and rationally understanding this concern with freedom has been of paramount importance through the modern period. In fact, it is an established concern in philosophy, and literature too projects this concern for individual freedom amply. Not so in India: our philosophers do not focus so much on what constitutes freedom or what its implications are, though in literature there is a clear and convincing portrayal of 'existential' themes in modern times. There is a school of critical thought, however, which regards such a feature as suspect or inauthentic in the Indian context. In Hindi as well as Urdu, I find a number of short stories presenting this existential approach. Would you say that this happened entirely due to the influence of western thought or can one discern the roots of such preoccupation with inwardness and self-realization in the Indian past?

MMA: Well, I wouldn't say new literature in India is inauthentic. There have been so many imperceptible changes here. And the consciousness of the educated class, not only of the elite segments of society, is very modern in this sense: it has taken ideas from the west and genuinely assimilated them. Also, because there have been a lot of social changes in India itself, those ideas do have reference to our social reality, too. The reason we are inclined to see them as unreal is that a large number of people are still illiterate. But even an illiterate factory worker (the proletariat class does exist) is facing that social reality which was unthinkable forty or fifty years ago - for example, he has to relate to his colleagues within a trade union, he has to relate to his family who make so many demands on him while his earnings are paltry. He also has to relate to his employers. The kind of social situation and social structure he's put into is a completely new phenomenon. He tries to cope with the new situation in his own way and feels frustrated. He does feel that alienation which our writers talk about. He himself may not be able to talk about his experience in those terms. He may not even be able to see in terms of those concepts, but that is a different matter. One has to carefully consider what and how people live and what they themselves make of their lives. They are not able to conceptualize the situation which actually does exist in modern existentialist terms. Our writers, who can conceptualize in those terms, have every right to do so. I wouldn't dismiss this as a borrowed phenomenon our lives are the referent. Of course modernization in literature has to reflect the modernization of society. A valid, authentic literature cannot hang in the air. But the changes in our literature do correspond with changes in society. Since the changes are slow, I think their appearance in literature is slow too.

S: Modern culture has to cope with quick changes driven by science and technology. Language too has to develop and keep pace with the movement. New expression has to evolve quickly. This may pose something of a problem for the writer. I imagine that the inclination to produce a 'literature of silence' emerged from just such a dilemma in post-modern literature. Not so in India. Such a dilemma does not seem to have been experienced here.

MMA: It is not that language itself fails to cope with the realities of new life, it is that any language, which is a symbolic representation of reality, has its limitations - doesn't matter how developed it is! And again, the expressed wish to escape the constraints of language to receive reality has connections with existential thought. The existentialists found existence unique and were compelled to think that it cannot be adequately represented in words. Sartre, for example, said that "existence overflows words", and that words cannot capture existence because existence is ever new. There's no essence of existence you can capture once and for all, or describe. The experience of 'getting choked' while using language, when you find existence is defying words, is part of this realization. So it does not matter how rich a language is; thus the search for new forms of expression outside language which could perhaps represent life better. But I think in India this kind of angst is not felt, perhaps because the pace of our lives is not that fast. Secondly, I don't subscribe to the idea that languages have not developed as much here. It's not the failure of particular languages. It is a desire to push the limits of language – and it could be the failure of particular writers to use language.

Language is not present as ready-made stuff to be used and applied to a situation; it is not just a dictionary of words. The creation of language, the creative use of language in literary writing, and the evolution of a social situation go hand in hand; the writer has a very important role to play. Writers add to the vocabulary; they create language.

S: Post-modernism is much discussed as a different intellectual, philosophical phenomenon following from modernism. How do you perceive post-modernism and what relationship do you see between modernism and post-modernism?

MMA: Well, I can talk about the general enlightenment behind post-modernism, which is really the full recognition of what we've learnt in modernism. Modernism consists of receiving the impact of the realization of freedom. Modernity means man's confrontation with freedom squarely. The modernist writer tried to cope with it. A few writers rejected it; others rejoiced in it and created new forms and new materials, rejecting the past. Some indeed were nostalgic for the past. The period of unease, when the writer is still groping with his new found freedom, is the period of modernity. What post-modernism gave us is no new form or theme or new philosophy as such, but only the realization that freedom is there once and for all, for good or for ill, and there's no going back from there. And that this freedom is absolute in the sense that it's all up to one's own self: how one lives, what one creates, and what one may offer as justification. I'd say that post-modernists have learned the art of living creatively with their freedom. Creativity is the psychic utilization of that freedom in time and space. I cannot identify or see any sort of descriptive theme or form in post-modernism. I only see the spirit of modernity fully realized and carried forward in full recognition of the fact of our freedom.

S: It is interesting to note that in India modernism and post-modernism are simultaneously present, while modernism is no longer visible in the west. In modernist literature value was accorded to abstraction as a non-acceptance of absolutes. Post-modernism does not even accept freedom as an absolute.

In literature, the traditional narrative form has re-emerged and reportage is a popular mode of expression. The effort is to describe the situation as it is but also at the same time realize that it is "perceived" to be so. What's to be presented then is the truth that is relative and not absolute. What may be seen as the truth can really be just one person's truth! The writer's self-reflexivity is acknowledged.

MMA: But when you say the writer reinstated old forms, there is a danger of misunderstanding post-modernism. Post-modernism does not consist of any attempt to bring something back. It is not a question of either reinstating or rejecting or accepting anything. It's absolute freedom, all the shackles have been thrown aside, whether in form or content. So nobody is going to tell the writer what to write, how to write, and so on.

S: The literary situation is rather complex here in India. So many approaches, styles, points of view, and literary philosophies exist simultaneously. On the one hand there is the modernist stance, the traditionalists are active too, and so are the avantgarde progressives. And now post-modernism too has emerged at the same time.

MMA: We are indeed open to many influences from outside in addition to having our own traditions and styles...

S: And yet we do have on the creative level a certain kind of a sensibility that synthesizes a lot of diversity. The modern world's so connected and small, everything's available to everyone...

MMA: It is not imitation that you witness in literature then…precisely because we do have the capacity to absorb anything new, to assimilate it into our own ways and then give our own meanings to it, eventually to make it our own. Post-modernism, which is a full realization of that freedom which brought about modernism, since it has come to India, frees us perhaps from the pains of trying to be modern for much longer.

S: A decisive point to conclude with! Thank you.

Ramesh Chandra Shah

On Hindi, the Short Story, and the 'Modern'

RAMESH CHANDRA SHAH

RAMESH CHANDRA SHAH (b. 1937) *was educated at Almora and at the University of Allahabad. He has taught English since 1960 as Professor and later Head of the Department of English at Hamidia College, Bhopal. Shah is a well-known poet and novelist in Hindi, critic, and recipient of several awards for his contributions to Hindi literature, including the* Shikhar-Samman *of the Madhya Pradesh government's Cultural Department (1988)*, and the Sahitya Akademi Award for his novel 'Vinayak' *in 2014. In addition to writings in Hindi Shah has published his doctoral dissertation on* Yeats and Eliot: Perspectives on India, *and a Sahitya Akademi monograph on Jai Shankar Prasad. Sponsored by the I.C.C.R. in 1978, he participated in the XVI International Writers' Conference in Belgrade. His published works include eleven novels such as* Gobar-Ganesh, Kissa Ghulam, *and* Poorvapar, *short story collections including* Jangal Mein Aag, Muhalle Ka Ravana, *and* Theatre and Manpatra, *poetry anthologies including* Kachchue Ki Pith Par, Harishchandra Aao, Nadi Bhagati Aai, *and critical works like* Chhayavad Ki Prasangikata, Samanantar, *and* Vagartha. *He has also published essay collections including* Shaitan Ki Bahane, Aduka Per, *and* Sabad Nirantar, *and a collection of lectures delivered at the Temenos Academy, London, titled* Ancestral Voices. *Shah is also a translator: his* Thus Spake

Bhartrihari *(Bhatrihari Satak) is a bilingual book – an English translation of the Diaries, Reminiscences, Travelogues, and Verse renderings of Bhartrihari.*

SUKRITA: Each age expresses its own imaginative construct of reality through the artist's creative consciousness. In that, I'd say art remains perhaps the one great sign of human freedom or indeterminacy. 'Modern' culture expresses itself in dams, bridges and factories and the features include the materialistic and down to earth, not the transcendent. They represent movement, change, and novelty. On the other hand a literary 'modernist' (in English literature Yeats, Eliot, Ezra Pound, Proust and such others) is not really engaged with technology and material progress. In fact literary modernism revels in the celebration of a renewable and knowable past. Thus the distinction between 'modernity' and 'modernism'. The crisis of reality necessitated, as it were, a reactive modernism. The romantic tendency to return to the past is a typical modernist stance. How do you understand this phenomenon particularly when a frenzied rebuilding of society and a discovery of a totally fresh condition of the human mind demanded a direct confrontation with the present?

RAMESH CHANDRA SHAH: Yes; a distinction between 'modernity' and 'modernism' is not entirely uncalled for; but I think it should be possible to do so without using categories like romanticism and classicism. We have to learn to do without them; particularly, when we seek to clarify our minds with regard to this issue in our own cultural context, where tradition has been accommodative enough to include both orthodoxy and heresy. The Indian mechanism of sensibility is perhaps not at all explicable in such terms.

Within the specific literary modernism you speak of, Eliot at first seemed most sympathetic to us with his very original and, to us, very appealing ideas about tradition. With all his anti-romantic stance, however, he now seems rather remote and not modern enough. On the other hand we find the avowedly 'romantic' Yeats much closer to our own way of apprehending the world, and in fact much more modern because of his heterodox but much more 'universal' sense of values. What our modern Indian mind finds most uncongenial in Eliot is precisely the unsuspected lure of orthodoxy concealed beneath his cosmopolitan sophistication. Yeats in comparison seems much more central and humane; his vision of humanity as well as the universe enveloping it is much more open and inclusive. And Joyce, I think, is much more modern and progressive than even Yeats. In fact his prose appears to unfold a vision of the future of mankind which is much more genuinely progressive than the so-called progressivism of politically motivated writers. This makes me doubt the validity of terms like 'reactionary' and 'progressive' too. Like 'romantic' and 'classical', they tend to act like traps rather than aids to thinking. Of course, each of the great modernists gave us valuable insights into reality. It is one of the strongest ironies of history that Eliot, the best modern interpreter of the idea of tradition, and in fact a leader of the modernist movement should have fallen into a trap which his historical consciousness itself should have protected him from. It is his kind of return to the past which, romantic or not, is authoritarian and anti-modern. Neither Arnold, the pre-modern, nor Saul Bellow, the post-modern could be called anti-modern in that sense.

The modern mind has rediscovered the value of the pagan and the pluralistic sensibility. It has also realized the limits of western tragic wisdom and is now groping its way towards a kind of holistic vision of life and death. This is something that the modernist movement failed to accomplish. It certainly deserves credit for creating a novel concept of tradition, and to that extent it has certainly become a vital part of our modern sensibility. You said that art remained perhaps the last sign of man's freedom or indeterminacy. Isn't it tragic that it should be so? Religion congealing into dogma and imperialism, philosophy becoming the abject surrender of the meditative before the calculative mind - what else could we have expected from such a dismal turn of events through the early twentieth century? That explains why Matthew Arnold - the pre-modernist who was in some ways a wiser man than the modernist Eliot - looked up to poetry as the future religion of mankind. "High destiny" indeed! But he, the last Greek and the admirer of Marcus Aurelius - "wandering between two worlds, one dead, the other powerless to be born" - is entirely without the prejudice and the complacency which appears so embarrassing amidst the achievement of the great modernists.

Conversion of the tragic into holistic wisdom: this is how a good part of the truly modern mind conceives its real concern; that is exactly where the Traditionalist and the Modern come closest to each other. That is the true perspective, in which not only the specific literary modernism you've mentioned falls into its proper place, but also the voice of an Arnold and a Saul Bellow: pre-modern and post-modern alike.

S: Modernity refers to time and linearity. It seems to refer to a significant suggestion of disconnection and loss of the past; it is also sometimes referred to as 'inverted traditionalism'. Conceptually what relationship do you see between tradition and modernity? The awareness of the 'present' seems at times to suggest the negation of the past. But I find the Hegelian, dialectical view of history very relevant here, which indicates how the human mind evolves historically and reality evolves with it. Modernism, therefore, is the realization of the dynamism of tradition. How do you respond to this?

RCS: That is an interesting idea: modernism seen as

'the realization of the dynamism of tradition' rather than as its negation or contradiction. Yes, I would rather agree. But not via Hegel. For Hegel, the rest of the world (that is, nine-tenths of the world) exists only for the sake of Europe or the European sense of the Spirit. He represents the culmination of that tendency in European philosophy which came to view the conceptual control of the universe as the only real task of philosophic thought. That was the road which led straight to Nietzsche's nihilist despair, and to ecological disaster confronting us.

The perception that the human mind evolves historically and reality evolves with it is certainly not the sole prerogative of Hegelian logic. Sri Aurobindo, for example, finds room for this historical logic even within his spiritual philosophy of the 'Life Divine'.

The Jungian "modern man in search of a soul" finds the religion and the philosophy of the self much more relevant than the Hegelian Absolute or the Hegelian or Marxian apotheosis of history. If modernity, as you say, refers to time and acquires a comparative stance it is the orthodox or the mainstream European-Christian view of time that is now felt to be sadly inadequate and inimical to man's quest for integration with the cosmos. The "cosmicomics" of a post-modernist fiction-writer like Italo Calvino or the sagas of a Marquez are examples of true modern creativity which disturb such complacent systems.

S: In Europe, a Nietzsche, a Marx, or a Freud caused tremendous upheavals in the thought-processes of society and in fact resulted in a radical transformation of people's world view and the human psyche. Here we've had a charismatic national leader, and rather pragmatic thinker, in Mahatma Gandhi. Would you say that the ideals Gandhi stood for have had a rather short-lived impact? Has it done anything to the

Indian psyche? How does Indian literature (particularly Hindi or Urdu fiction) demonstrate his impact?

RCS: The ideas that Gandhi stood for are centrally related to that holistic Indian vision of life and universe which I was trying to connect with the real quest behind the wanderings of the modern mind. It won't do to look upon him as just a charismatic national leader; and his being a pragmatic rather than a speculative thinker is exactly what makes him much more relevant and much more responsible than Marx. If the human mind evolves historically and reality evolves with it then the two points of growth in modern Indian history are unmistakably represented by Sri Aurobindo and Mahatma Gandhi; just as the parallel points of growth are represented in European history by Nietzsche and Marx. They are the Indian equivalents of those two great shapers of the modern European mind. Compare them and you'll find that both Gandhi and Sri Aurobindo are much more forward-looking, much more radically and responsibly transformative than their European counterparts. As for their "short-lived impact", the reason is evident in what the philosopher K. C. Bhattacharya called our failure to achieve *swaraj* in ideas. The Indian mind, according to this acute thinker, has become a shadow mind. Hindi literature acquires a modern voice with Bhartendu Harishchandra, but he wrote no fiction. The modern sensibility in prose is inaugurated through the essays of Balmukund Gupta, who shows historical awareness and weaves past and present in a significant pattern. The impact of Gandhi on Hindi fiction has been very widespread and deep. The late Jainendra Kumar - the subtlest and the deepest amongst modern fiction writers was creatively a close interpreter of the Gandhian vision.

In fact, the impact of Gandhi on Indian fiction has been more pervasive than any other phenomenon. But the best examples are those in which it works indirectly: Raja Rao's *Kanthapura,* for example. You have to note that it's not the so-called Gandhian ideology that matters there. True to tradition, Gandhi himself declined to bequeath a clear-cut ideology. He could easily have done so; others have tried to do it; but his extraordinary spiritual common sense prevented him from attempting any such thing, and he was right. You cannot reduce life to a logical process. Reductionist ideology is the most characteristic and the most rampant evil besetting the modern mind. It is anti-traditional and anti-modern. It is bound to work against what you call man's freedom or indeterminacy. In fact, Gandhi and Sri Aurobindo - otherwise so different from each other - are both alike in one respect: they cannot be reduced to an ideology, as Nietzsche and Marx certainly can be.

An artist's relationship with a thinker or leader of men is bound to be ambivalent. It can be simple and straightforward, as it was during Gandhi's own lifetime. Then his presence elicited extremes of adulation or hatred. Some of the most talented fiction writers who evinced indifference or hostility to him at one point have now come closer to his vision than Gandhians themselves. This kind of creative relationship with Gandhi has started gaining ground now, and it is a very significant development of recent years. Another thing that attracts our notice is that even the most avowedly Gandhian among fiction writers –Jainendra Kumar - is a free and creative interpreter of the Gandhian vision rather than the purveyor of an ideology.

S: Modernity is generally identified with industrialization or Westernization. I would say that Lloyd and Susanne Hoeber Rudolphs' suggestion that potential of traditional societies be analyzed and identified in order to understand the phenomenon of modernization is crucial. The persistence of traditional features within modernity would mean surer, stable cultural contexts and the creative expression of such a feature would not necessitate radically different and rather sensational formalistic experimentation. I wonder if the thesis presented in *The Modernity of Tradition* (1969) partly explains why we do not see this dramatic avantgarde tendency in Indian literature – whether the sense of tradition is never lost.

RCS: Yes, in spite of the drift and disorientation - in spite of the omnipresent corruption and absence of work-ethic -it does seem to me that Indian society has much more in-built resistance and resilience than any other Eastern society. Here is a paradox: no people in the world have shown as much sympathetic understanding of the West as we have done. The Indian mind has an uncanny capacity for entering other modes of apprehending the world; the Indian sensibility has what Keats called 'negative capability'. On the other hand, this negative capability is itself the other side of an affirmative capability assured of its centrality and humanity. The Japanese or the Chinese may outwardly appear to be more consciously careful of their Japanese or Chinese identity; they may have preserved certain forms of family and communal life in better shape; but we know that they have proved inwardly very vulnerable to the onslaught of the imperialistic modern West. The crisis there may well be deeper than it is here. It is very easy to achieve quick results in economic and political spheres with a homogeneous people that has been accustomed to more or less imperialistic regimes and who can easily combine feudal loyalty with modern technological organization. But the problem of forging a modern unity out of such diversity and plurality as we have to work within our country is incomparably more challenging.

Of course we do witness the persistence of traditional features within the fast-changing life around us. Indian civilization seems to have accepted the great dialectical challenge of the West without compromising its integrity.

There have been signs of conflict in the Indian psyche right from the beginning, reflected in the controversy that arose between Tagore and Gandhi, Gandhi and M.N. Roy, and last but not least, between Gandhi and Nehru. It is a pity that the last and the most crucial of these dialogues could never really take place. Was it not a marriage of incompatibles from the very beginning? We can say that Nehru was Gandhi's anti-self or creative mask, as the West in general is India's anti-self and creative mask. I am using this Yeatsian terminology knowingly and deliberately; it was not a sterile relationship. Obviously Gandhi felt some sort of an elective affinity with Nehru precisely because he was different and capable of independent thinking in spite of his orientation toward the Western mode of living and thinking. Only a profoundly religious soul could have had such confidence in an agnostic. After all, the leader of the masses had to come to terms with the leader of the intelligentsia somewhere. Well, Gandhi was extremely realistic and he had experienced an early disillusionment with the real character of Indian intelligentsia: he called it "hard-hearted"; he felt it to be "the constant nightmare of his life". And yet he had to make his choice amongst the availables. He chose Nehru; what else could he have done? He chose Nehru and almost in the same breath he advised the Congress party to dissolve itself, to become a grass-roots organization of dedicated workers for national reconstruction at every level of society; knowing well that this was the last thing to be expected from Nehru.

Yes; no sensational formalistic experimentation was called for in our case: but creative, life-giving experiment was essential. The creation of modern Hindi language and literature itself was - from one point of view - the most daring of experiments. Hindi had to act as the cultural clearing house in its new incarnation as well. Hence the new writing in it - the most creative core of it had to find itself through quiet experimentation. Hence it is that the best writers were innovators and experimentalists in the early part of their career; later, having found themselves, they naturally could afford to become confidently and self-assuredly traditional. We did not need to take such drastic measures as Eliot and Joyce did. Our situation was very different. Centuries of political and cultural humiliation had not reduced culture itself to broken fragments. The problem was one of renewal and reconstruction rather than one of doomsday judgment. If we lacked the European vision of evil, as Yeats thought we did, our psyche was comparatively free from guilt as well. Why is Premchand's *Godaan* superior as a work of modern Hindi fiction to Yashpal's *Jhootha Sach*? Both are documentary, panoramic novels with a lot of period-flavour that has worn off with time. Both deal with areas of darkness in the modern Indian milieu. Both give us social realism. How is it then, that I can still remember and visualize so much of the life and character in *Godaan,* while I retain little of the other novel? I think it is primarily because of the active presence of tradition in Premchand's world. The ancestral voice could still be heard within it, in spite of the rumblings of change, in spite of the positively realized desirability of change in the old rural world. The sense of tradition is never lost even in the comparatively iconoclastic world of Jainendra and Agyeya. The latter's fiction was motivated by the 'search for individuality'. But even his most 'existential' novel *Apne Apne Ajnabi* reveals a consciousness deeply imbued with the traditional Indian sense of values. Here is an interesting case: a writer adopting a rebel's, an outsider's, stance and becoming an insider. He becomes the Other to return with greater certainty to himself. Again and again it has been proved that tradition reasserts itself through the creative individual who risks his security within it. Although Agyeya stopped writing fiction, his poetry demonstrates this 'homecoming' most triumphantly.

The Sixties and Seventies did witness some sensational formalistic experimentation as well. Since most of it was derivative, uninspired by any genuine crisis or quest, nobody remembers it now. But a few stories by Gyanranjan, Vinod Kumar Shukla, Usha Priyamvada and Kashinath Singh still survive because they opened up new areas of sensibility and gave new insights into changing relationships in society. Their linguistic structural novelty did answer some real needs.

S: If you were to analyse the intellectual situation of the first three decades in India offer partition would you say that it agrees with the perception of the sense of void, of intellectual nullities, expressed in English literature from the first three decades of the twentieth century? The spiritual paralysis, death of metaphysics, lost sense of direction, failure of communication, etc.? Is the horror of Partition analogous with the horror of the World Wars?

RCS: No, the intellectual situation in India is not at all similar to that expressed by English literature in the early twentieth century. I do not mean that all is well with us. I repeat what I've said already about the lack of *swaraj* in ideas: it is a failure to confront and define our situation in depth. Our philosophers have not responded to the challenge; our writers lack the will to face up to the task. It's not a failure of communication; it's not the death of metaphysics; it is a lack of courage to face the void in oneself and see beyond it. The way they tend to conceive of and resolve their problems within the Marxist or the existentialist framework of ideas leads one to suspect that though they may be sincere their sincerity is not enough; they are availing themselves of structures and solutions which they themselves know only at second hand. This makes our literary modernism too literary.

The horror of Partition produced *Jhootha Sach* and some very poignant stories by Agyeya and others. I once asked a very talented Kannada writer whether anything had been written on this theme in his language. He could not remember anything of the sort. Which raises a disturbing question in my mind: Are we really incapable of facing and coming to terms with evil? Is it our total disregard of history? Or is this a call to question the Indian union: what sort of unity is that which can afford to be so hopelessly localized? And that leads me too to the unbridgeable gap between the great manifestations of an aristocratic-spiritual culture and the deaf and dumb millions. Who is to blame then, except the hard-hearted intelligentsia: the middlemen of culture who usurp all benefits in every new regime and are answerable to none! They reap the benefits of tradition as well as of modernity without creatively contributing anything to either.

S: Modernism then may be seen as particularly urban and metropolitan, maintaining a distance from local origins and class allegiances, family, race, or religion. There is also a movement toward secularization, impersonality, and universalization. However, all realities seem to become subjective in the specific delineation of particular situations and characters. The writer's major concern (as in the case of his western counterpart) is the dehumanization of modern man (as in Charlie Chaplin's *Modern Times*). There seems a search for the universal in the occluded wilds of the 'personal'. How would you compare the urban modern writer of the West with any from here? Are there major differences of sensibility?

RCS: I once divided modern fiction writers into two categories. To the first belonged writers whose imagination seemed well-rooted in the life of the community. They did concern themselves with changes in family relationships owing to increasing self-assertion in individual members, the loosening of the joint family system, etc. In the second category I placed those who were concerned with the 'emancipated' fringe of society, seeking various refinements of isolation, distortion, psychological disorders, etc. I have a feeling that the *kind* of personality which is the product of the Indian family system and ethos is intrinsically different from its European counterpart. Here an individual grows among a network of relationships and is rather slow to achieve individuality. There the growth of individual identity is quicker. Personality and privacy are more valuable in the West. The pattern of our emotional development is very different. Modern education tends to encourage feelings of independence and sharpened individuality. But with most of us it is a spurious feeling. For example, the family network guarantees emotional security to most of us. Yet we like to feign insecurity. Dishonest and hypocritical attitudes are bound to appear in our behaviour as well as in our writings. Fiction- especially the novel - requires interesting individualized characters and their deep awareness of inner life. Sometimes I ask myself how it is that the short story rather than the novel seems to suit the Indian mind better. Is it because the original form of the novel centres inescapably in and around the individual while the short story is basically a social form needing just people - a community of listeners. Not sharply individuated persons. I am not sure.

The morally responsible individual having to contend with an indifferent or self-seeking milieu is the theme of some good stories by Agyeya and Nirmal Verma. The lonely individual hankering after a relationship and maladjusted couples occupy the centre of Mohan Rakesh's stories. Rajendra Yadav, too, among other things, concerns himself with the close delineation of various psychological complexes and consequent distortions in individuals. Kamleshwar too depicts the change that follows in a character brought up in the close-knit society of a small town who has now been drawn into the vortex of a big city. The abrupt transition from a rural to an urban life occupies so many modern Hindi stories that this itself could be looked upon as the clearest symptom of modernity in Indian fiction. But let me tell you, the most genuine and sensitive stories of this change have come from the pen of Phanishwar Nath 'Renu', who has also produced two authentically Indian novels of post-independence Indian society and character.

One may note that these maladjusted individuals, in spite of the various distortions induced in them by modern life, still do belong to a more or less recognizably homogenized culture. But without serious concern with the roots of this culture and without extreme sensitiveness to and knowledge of the character of 'modern' complexity, the depiction of the problem tends to remain superficial. It reduces your fiction to a rather sentimental version of psychological curiosity or social realism. If you want your critique of life to go deeper you have to show a deeper and subtler awareness of human comedy or tragedy. It is here that the work of K.B. Vaid, with his tough metaphysical despair and unrelentingly serious preoccupation with the inner and outer squalor of individual and communal life acquires special relevance.

S: Who do you regard as your favourite modern short-story writers in India?

RCS: If I restrict myself to the area of Hindi fiction, the names that occur to me are Agyeya, Jainendra Kumar, Nirmal Verma, Kunwar Narain, Raghubir Sahai, Usha Priyamvada, Phanishwarnath 'Renu', Bhishma Sahni, Amarkant, Shekhar Joshi, Prayag Shukla, Gyan Ranjan, G.M. Muktibodh and K.B. Vaid. On the whole, with the exceptions of Renu and Vaid, it is the poets who have grappled best with modern ideas and produced technically interesting and significant stories. Kunwar Narain and Raghubir Sahai have certainly broken new ground here. Kunwar Narain's stories are outstanding in their novel treatment of ideas. He exhibits the moral and intellectual ambivalence of modern life and thought in his stories. Muktibodh is very sensitive in his delineation of self-alienated characters, whose self-alienation is the inevitable outcome of their self-seeking adjustments and betrayals of their own conscience.

S: At what point in the history of the Hindi short-story would you say that 'modernism' emerged? Do you think 'existentialism' - a major philosophical base of the 'modern' Western psyche - influenced our writers authentically enough for the 'existential' story to emerge in its own right and full strength in Hindi? The modern Hindi short story writer (particularly Nirmal Verma, Krishna Baldev Vaid, Gyan Ranjan, Kashinath Singh) projects a sensibility that accommodates existential despair, the 'absurd', and awareness of the dichotomy between illusion/appearance and reality. There is an attempt to explore the subconscious. Though the philosophic base is apparently Western, these perspectives can be located in our own Vedic and Upanishadic literature. Do you think the assimilation of these ideas is really an evocation of the 'unconscious' in the Indian writer?

RCS: Well, I can't give the exact date but it was perhaps somewhere in early fifties or late forties that Agyeya wrote those famous stories called *Kothari ki baat, Hili bon ki Batthaken* and *Gangrene.* In the academic world, it has been customary to regard the publication of *Gangrene* as the decisive turning point, where the Hindi short story came to evince a distinctly modernist sensibility.

No doubt Agyeya, with his new emphasis on the search for individuality, deserves credit for inaugurating a new kind of self-consciousness - also a brand new language to explore areas of human personality which had hitherto not engaged the attention of Hindi writers of fiction. But even this pioneer had a predecessor in Jainendra Kumar, who, in spite of his deep links with Gandhian ways of experimenting with personal and social truth, or perhaps because of that very serious involvement, had quite spontaneously opened up these possibilities in Hindi fiction. He was not a very conscious artist; in fact he always repudiated the idea of a conscious artist. One can even sense a Lawrentian anti-intellectualist stance in his attitudes. But his writing has always had a disturbing impact. Take his novel *Tyagpatra* for example. It has been very ably translated into English by Agyeya himself as *Resignation.* It is perhaps the shortest novel ever written in any Indian language: the shortest and most intense. You could almost read it like a long short story though your reading experience, the depths of human suffering you touch in the story, the almost Dostoievskian intensity of its revolt and surrender, make you feel that only a novel proper could do all this to you: such a deep and at the same time wide-ranging communication is beyond the scope of a short story. And he has written short stories as well, which sound utterly different from the work of his mentor Premchand. To name just a few - *Patni, Ek Raat, Neelam Deshki Rajkanya*. You can see the struggle of traditional existence with modern ideas in such stories.

Existentialism? Well, Agyeya's *Kothari ki baat* is the first widely read existentialist story to have been published in Hindi. It is no mere coincidence that his last fictional work too has an existentialist theme. But no sensitive reader of this novel *Apne Apne Ajnabi* can fail to perceive that the atmosphere, the treatment of this theme, is wholly Indian. It is a personally realized vision of a threshold experience and there is nothing even remotely derivative in the feeling or the writing. Of the other writers you have listed, K.B.Vaid comes closest to existentialist sensibility. His fiction had a somewhat naturalistic beginning in its obsessive preoccupation with inner and outer squalor. The attempt to express subconscious feelings becomes very evident in Vaid's world. In fact, he seems to be one of the most modern and experimental of Hindi fiction writers.

He explores extremes of subjectivity and self-awareness and is unique in his unrelenting pursuit. There is a groping towards some sort of design in this obsession with the sordid particulars of existence: there is always the same protagonist analysing, revealing, pursuing his own image. Nowhere else do we see such an extended motif of the double, such a dogged, desperate compulsion to sift reality from appearance. But it is always more and more appearance. Reality is forever receding, elusive, and even self-defeating. There are no glimmerings of eternal design, or epiphanies. But there certainly appears an integrity of despair and self-defeat refusing to seek premature resolution of conflict or reconciliation with the inevitable. As for the philosophic base, Vaid's fiction is apparently closer to the Western modes than to what you choose to call Vedic or Upanishadic. From a literary view point too, it is akin to Joyce and Beckett rather than to any ancient or modern Indian examples. It makes Vaid's writing utterly unlike Agyeya's, or even Muktibodh's.

Nirmal Verma could not be called an existentialist in that sense; though the kind of seriousness he brought to Hindi fiction does have that flavour. Love, man-woman relationships, is his primary theme as well as his means of exploring reality. His preoccupation with the loneliness and desolation of individual lives defines his modernity. But he is not as overtly modernist and experimental like his contemporary Vaid. His basic conflict is between innocence and experience. His imagination is obsessed with "remembrance of things past". He depicts relationships that have either been broken or are in the process of crumbling. His characters do not have solid ground beneath their feet. Love is frustrating rather than fulfilling. The Other is congenial and sympathetic only when he is a real Other and utter stranger. There is no happiness or meaning in traditionally stable relationships, those between father and son, or husband and wife.

But if Verma's world is a world of unstable relationships threatened from within and without it is still a world of relationships, no matter how tragic or unsatisfactory. It is quite unlike the world of K.B. Vaid, which connects nothing with nothing-a world of non-relation, or a provisional pattern of reality. Relations seem to arise from and dissolve into the ever-present, ever-threatening void. With Verma on the other hand, the need to relate, however doomed to frustration, is still the overwhelming need. Need to relate not only with the Other as the Other, but also with the Other as one's own self. And a Nirmal Verma character feels this overwhelming need to relate not just with the human but also with sub-human, supra-human, and natural worlds. In fact, Verma seems to have realized the futility of seeking meaning only through the rather romantically oriented longing to love and possess the Other. Later he seemed to be groping towards a holistic sense of community with all; that seemed the only way to transcend the inevitable frustrations of love and longing. Not that this aspiration, this necessity to transcend, had been satisfactorily realized, but the preliminary self-knowledge seemed already achieved in some stories of his collection *Kawwe Aur Kalapani.* Shapes of death still haunt his characters; there is salvation neither for the world-renouncing brother, nor for the one struggling in the world below those heights, but the right to self-determination is acknowledged. Of course, a certain ironic deflation of the instinct, to withdraw, can be seen operating in the story. But it is not presented as mere feeble-minded escape. There is sympathetic insight as well as irony in the depiction of this recluse. And he gained some sort of wry wisdom as well. He earned the moral right to criticise the possessive greed of the brother at home. I mention this story because it is a significant departure from the recognisedly modernist despair and loneliness of his earlier stories. The questioning, the doubt, had grown deeper here though it had not as yet acquired that metaphysical resonance which seems to distinguish a truly great modern story.

Yes, I do believe that existential perspectives can be located in and recaptured from our own Vedic and Upanishadic literature too. But I cannot confidently assert that a real evocation of the unconscious in these terms and in this sense has so far been witnessed in any Indian fictional writing. We are poised to attain something of the sort now; that is all one can safely assume.

S: How would you define 'modernism' in the context of the Hindi story? What is the writer's approach to language? In writers such as Beckett, Borges, etc. there is a loss of faith in the word as an effective vehicle of meaning. The inadequacy of human language is shown through making words set in proper grammatical structures look redundant and absurd. Does the contemporary Hindi writer show such a concern?

RCS: There have been lots of significant experiments and innovations in the Hindi story which would have been impossible without the modernist movement on a global scale. The loss of faith in the word itself is not, truly speaking, our problem. I do not think any significant Hindi writer has ever been much concerned with such a predicament. The language we write in is a brand new reincarnation of the medieval lingua franca and is yet to realize its best potentialities. There is no question of exhaustion here.

Moreover we are not a guilt-ridden people. In spite of all the humiliations heaped upon us by history, we and our speech are comparatively innocent and fresh. I have already pointed out the significant work done by Agyeya, Muktibodh, K.B. Vaid, and Nirmal Verma- the explorers of modern consciousness. It goes without saying that each of them has achieved a lot by way of experimentation and innovation in technique and form because each one of them has had things to say that were genuine expressions of "modern man in search of a soul".

Krishna Sobti

"On the Autonomy of the Writerly Self"
-Extracts from Conversations

KRISHNA SOBTI

KRISHNA SOBTI is one of the most significant writers of modern India. In 1980 she was awarded the Sahitya Akademi award for her novel Zindaginama and *the Sahitya Akademi* Fellowship *was given to her in 1996. For her contribution to Indian literature she was also awarded the Jnanpith Award in 2017. A writer with a distinctly outspoken demeanour, she responded to and wrote constantly on contemporary socio-political scene, recording her comments on the times she lived in. Her literary output came out of an angst to create characters who carve their destiny in dignity. Her first novel Channa was published as her last novel, if only because she would not compromise on the language of the novel which the publisher tried to modified when she first approached him. Her novels have been translated in several languages.*

My conversations with Krishna Sobti in the last three years of her life were frequent and unusually intense. During this period she was in and out of the hospital with serious bouts of ill health that perhaps led to her rather nervous concern that time was running out. She was keen to use her time well to consolidate her writings, her intellectual as well as material possessions, as also a whole lot of her life experiences vibrating in her bountiful memories. Though extremely private about the nature of her illness, it seemed as if she felt compelled for a greater sharing than ever before, of her ideas and responses to the present times as well as the memories and experiences of the past. She had always resisted talking about her health issues and needed to be constantly persuaded by her companion and caretaker, Vimlesh, to attend to her physical ailments. Sharply alert about time moving on and conscious about her ageing self, she seemed to acquire greater energy to go down the memory lane on the one hand and on the other, become acutely attentive to the present-day political environs and its social impact.

Krishna Sobti had an inimitable style of narrating an incident. Never would one feel that she may be recalling something from as long back as seventy or more years ago. In the very process of narrating an incident or a story, she relived every moment as though it were happening in that moment itself. The eyes sparkling with a glint and her cheeks swelling with a chuckle in her mouth, with a small indication of a likely twist in her tale, she embarked upon the telling of the tale as though confessing some naughty deed of hers lying in secrecy within her. One such story was that of her horse ride of 1943, when as a young lady of eighteen, she conspired with the horseman Nawab Babu, and without telling her mother, got on the saddle of a horse to travel back home on a horse. Her eyes danced in delight as she went on to describe how she fell off the horse along with the saddle when he joggled in excitement on sighting a mare drinking water at a pond yonder. She broke her ankle but concealed it from the mother till much later!

But that is so characteristic of Krishna ji, the one who was a storyteller par excellence precisely because she was able to store so much in the secret recesses of her memory and then she'd make a selective and creative use of the rich repertoire discreetly. She spent long hours alone with herself in darkness, night after night, exploring her mind and adding to the research required for the imaginative reconstruction of stories she planned to write. Her conversation demonstrated her vast reading of classics in English as well as in translation from different parts of the world and of course she kept herself informed about contemporary Hindi writers and their writings. The first book that she ever read she said was on Napoleon Bonaparte's wife, followed by the memoires of Napoleon himself. She confessed how she was for some reason fond of reading war novels, perhaps because she felt intrigued by the conspiratorial planning that went into the making of wars in the world. Many a time she referred to James Baldwin's *Another Country* with great warmth and passion and recommended it fervently as a modern classic. Her comments on other people's writings were always very interesting. Once when Namwar Singh asked her to comment on Swadesh Deepak's novel *Maine Mandu Nahin Dekha*, she responded, "this is the sick man's most healthy book."

Often in informal conversations with Krishna ji, I had the fortune of travelling back to the times when the literary scene for modern fiction in Hindi was at its zenith. As a storyteller is adept to do, she would describe in detail her interactions with literary stalwarts who were actually, along with her, making history through their vibrant fiction while writing with a new post-Independence sensibility. New

Hindi journals and magazines were getting established. Those were the "happening" times for literature in Hindi and many other Indian languages. A remarkable tableaux of iconic and legendary writers such as Agyeya, Nirmal Verma, Krishan Baldev Vaid, Bhisham Sahni, Kamleshwar ran before my eyes as Krishna ji would narrate anecdotes that yielded important insights into their works and times. Some of the pieces in the series of sketches by Krishna ji in *Hum Hashmat* emerge from these times.

In the last few years of her life, many times Krishna ji voiced her keen desire to write a piece on Kapila Vatsyayan as part of her *Hum Hashmat* series. I witnessed how she agonized about not having done adequate research on this iconic personality to whom she felt so attracted. The fourth volume of the series was published just about a month before she passed away but she could not somehow write on Kapila ji. Writing about her contemporaries, commenting also on socio-political issues and recording her experiences of literary parties and get togethers, Krishna Sobti had worked out a different style and a distinct voice for these volumes. The sketches in *Hum Hashmat* demonstrate the writer's extraordinary alertness with which she discerned people and her environs; she chose to write these series in the male voice. This was perhaps used as a strategy to free herself as from gender biases; she acquired a distinctly different voice and style for *Hum Hashmat*. It may be pertinent to mention here that she often discussed with me the concept of androgyny for writers, as defined by Virginia Woolf. She never wished to be confined to the female gender as a writer. As she stepped into the role of Hashmat, she said often, her personality transformed and her began writing differently .

When I brought Kapila Vatsyayan to Krishna Sobti's flat in Mayur Vihar less than two years ago, I became acutely aware of the unusual energy each one reflected while involved in a fervent dialogue on contemporary times. While both of them deeply engaged with the present moments, each carried the baggage of a rich past. Not them, to be indulging in the nostalgia of the times gone by, nor did they involve themselves in constructing merely futuristic dreams…they were engaged with the 'here and now' enthusiastically. Even this hour-long intense conversation was clearly not adequate for Krishna ji to do her piece on Kapila ji. I brought to her Jyoti Sabharwal's book, *Kapila Vatsyayan: A Cognitive Biography,* and skimmed through all of it with her but somehow whatever she may have sought was not to be found! And Krishna ji was not able to write her piece till the end. Indeed, it was to do with some creative urge to resolve something about a character or a situation that compelled her to write a novel, or even a piece for her book of sketches.

The restlessness to write notwithstanding, Krishna Sobti was not a writer who was impatient to publish after she finished with a novel or a story. Like bricks, words had to remain in the kiln till they were absolutely ready to be delivered. There was never a hurry to publish. As she told me, usually she created three drafts of any novel, before sending it off for publication. The second draft usually changed radically into becoming something else but the third draft almost always went back to acquiring the shape of the first one! The process had to be gone through anyway, for the writer to feel content with the manuscript.

Not so in the case of her first novel entitled *Channa.* That ironically became her last published novel. This novel came out recently in January 2019, in the very last days of her life when she was in the hospital. Written more than six decades ago, she had withdrawn this novel from the publisher on discovering that the editors had changed the language of the novel here and there. Sobti bought all the published copies then, burnt them and put away the original manuscript of the novel locked in a trunk for decades. Her other works kept getting written and published over the years, but not this one. She had always wanted to get back to *Channa* for a fresh look before giving it to a new publisher. A perfectionist, as also an extremely patient reader and editor of her own work, she did not want it to be published as it was. When in the hospital last year, she had to be persuaded to get it out of the trunk. Earlier, no one - absolutely no one - could challenge her writerly decisions, not even her own self when not in the creative mode. It would be pertinent to recall here a remark she made to me about the cover of *Channa*: "Amrita Shergil's painting on the cover is beautiful. It is, I believe, much better than the novel between the covers." I think this remark came out of a tinge of unhappiness she suffered in not being able to revise the manuscript as she desired before its publication. She had given in…It must be noted that this is not a judgement on the novel as it exists now but I narrate this only to highlight the writer's persistent wish to re-look at the manuscript as a perfectionist. She was perhaps too weak to take on the project of the revision of the novel at this stage and thus, even though she succumbed to the persuasion so uncharacteristically, to publish it, she used her pragmatic discretion to have the book out.

The autonomy Krishnaji cherished for her own self, gets amply reflected in her characters too. The pulsating characters of her novels demand the 'dignity of being' in the same way as she sought for herself. She fiercely guarded this dignity for her self as also for her characters. Be it Mitro of *Mitro Marjani* or Mehak and Kutumb of *Dilo Danish*, or the mother and the daughter of *Ay Ladki* and many of her other characters, each one acquires a distinct identity as an individual. Each one cherishes her own desires and each one wishes to carve out her own life. Even though the mother and the daughter in *Ay Ladki* remain in dialogue with each other throughout, each maintains her own specific voice. As for the writer's own unique voice, as she often remarked, in order to write she needed to be constantly attentive to the inner voice which she could hear most clearly in the darkness of the night. Sleeping through the daytime and fully awake at night, she was completely receptive to the call from the inner being. Krishna Sobti spent her nights at her desk which was in fact like a sacred altar to her. "In some blessed moment, creation knocks at the inner being of the writer…a writer's insight searches immortality for human existence in the eternity of this world" - So said Krishna Sobti in a voice that seemed to emerge from some deep well of experience. She was a wordsmith who weaved words meticulously with great skill into fiction that told more truth than reality itself, agonising over each phrase, a word and it sound too. Each of her novels is a complete universe unto itself.

As for her magnum opus, *Zindaginama*, this is a novel that fetched Krishna ji the Sahitya Akademi Award. And this novel, most deservedly. The novel tells the tale of a whole age, an epic saga of times that could be showcased as the culmination of an evolving composite culture of the Indian subcontinent. This brings to mind the Urdu writer Qurratulain Hyder's celebrated novel *Aag ka Darya*. In both these novels, it was the apocalyptic division of the country that triggered the creative urge in these writers to recall the macro story of shared cultures that grew so naturally on this soil. *Zindaginama* evocatively presents a large socio-cultural canvas filled with different but shared myths, legends, festivals and beliefs but also minor quarrels and strife amongst varied classes, men and women and communities in the rural setting of Gujarat/ Punjab. There is no single protagonist, or a villain and the novel is peopled by a large number of persons. While Hyder's novel spreads over a large range of time, Sobti's offers a microscopic and detailed cultural mapping of a rich geographical domain. In both, there is extraordinary artistic skill and energy at work, in innovating fresh language and style to narrate a history pertinent specifically to the post-Partition Subcontinent right up to contemporary times. The truths unravelled by the authors of such range of vision serve as guiding forces in the very living of lives in communal togetherness. The emphasis is on an empathetic understanding and then respect for differences amongst people. Harmony is possible only where there is respect for difference: that seems to be the vital message to be taken from such a sensitive portrayal of the cultural negotiations presented through life experience in *Zindaginama.*

For many a writer, the pain of Partition has been difficult to express. Krishna ji lived with that anguish till her end but at different points of time she kept reverting to the theme of Partition in a variety of ways. Her autobiographical narration of the experience of Partition found its way earlier in three chapters of *Gujarat Pakistan se, Gujarat Hindustan* published as three episodes in the Hindi magazine "Tadbhav" from Lucknow several years before she actually developed the same into a larger narration which got published in 2017. The wounds of history on her personal self slowly find expression and gather in this book of which she herself is the protagonist, a refugee who was in search of a home after losing it on the other side of the border. "We are like sharpened knives…We have ourselves become weapons"…Having lost everything during the violence of the riots, what seemed to remain in the survivors is a fire for at times revenge and at times to ignite new life; it lies inside seething with helpless anger. Sobti's writing arouses the desire to return to humanity. As with BhishamSahni's novel *Tamas* or Kamleshwar's *Kitne Pakistan* and several other Partition writings, there is a compelling humanism and a moral dimension injected subtly and indirectly. Sometimes through the sheer depiction of the gruesome and irrational violence witnessed during the 1947 upheaval, what is evoked is a deep repulsion for such anti-human conduct by men of both communities. While writers such as Saadat Hasan Manto were writing immediately after Partition, many writers wrote about it much later, perhaps to escape the imaginative reliving of the tragedy that happens in the very process of writing.

In February 2018, in a conversation with me, Krishna ji spoke about how "distance can create another kind of familiarity. When you are writing", she said "you have to maintain a distance and yet remain in intimate proximity with what you are depicting; there is a distance but a measured one. If you are too close, you forget about the otherness of the phenomenon. There is thus a collapse of the binary of what is called subjectivity and objectivity. Though the otherness is not that of the writer, it has to be dealt with." As a writer, she explained, you become an insider/outsider, a witnessing self from the outside but you also remain a participant. She defined this as a very delicate predicament of the writer who can go over the edge. What may be already in the mind acquires a new look in a flash. This moment does not come dramatically though. One needs to recognize such a moment and hold on to it or else it may just slip by. "You are actually disturbed by this flash moment; you have to know how to handle that disturbance or you fail miserably," she continued "That's when poetry happens". This reminds me of the two lines of poetry she recited to me, written by her as a child in school at Shimla: "*Main muskarati si subah, darti hui si shaam hoon; Main mitnewalon ka yugon tak rhnewala vo naam hoon.*" ("I am that somewhat smiling dawn, I am that somewhat frightened evening; I am that name from amongst the mortals, which will live for centuries"). These lines won her a silver medal!

Whenever Krishnaji talked about her childhood days at Shimla where her family would move with the British to the summer capital in the pre-Independence times, she would slip into the dreamy world of clouds, mountains and the blue open skies. Her eyes twinkling, she described the skating scenes of Shimla with people waltzing delightfully on the glittering white ice! She'd pause reflecting on the pure blue of the sky, her eyebrows tilting in nostalgia. And then suddenly she remembered how she witnessed the long procession on the Lower Bazaar for the adoption of Hindi as an official language in India in late 1940's. She added, "there was a protest too on the Upper Mall." All this was going on while the War propaganda by the British was full on. Her family stayed in Gulshan Lodge when they were in Shimla. "Ha ha , you know what," she would chuckle, "when I was brought into this world in 1925, that's when the railcar was brought to Shimla." Each one, I thought quietly, was unique, and she definitely much more!

Krishna Sobti's book on Ladakh vouches for the deep love she experienced for the Himalayas. Her book *Buddha ka Kamandal Ladakh* captures the vibrancy of the colourful rocks of the wondrous landscape of Ladakh in its narration and indeed through photographs. The writer's ardent love for Himalayas finds expression in both word as well as deed. She would tirelessly share her experiences of trekking on these mountains as also those of Uttaranchal, specially around Mukteshwar. Krishna ji relished the idea of establishing direct and experiential contact with what she admired, the aesthetics of nature. She had no qualms in making bold choices about her travels, both in her mind as well as physically.

Soon after she married the Dogri writer Shiv Nath ji at the age of seventy, Krishna ji and I spent an evening of conversation and celebration at India International Centre.

Surprisingly, she had married someone born on the same date and year as herself, 18th February 1925! It was clear that she respected and admired Shiv Nath ji ardently. They had decided to live together, go through the process of aging together and some practical compulsions led to their decision of sealing this relationship with official stamp of marriage. Reflecting on their decision and the nature of their relationship, Krishna ji felt compelled to explore and articulate her thoughts through the writing of her novel *Samay Sargam.* In this book, the wisdom and maturity of sharing the process of 'aging' finds expression between the covers in a very calm and serene fashion. Vasudha Dalmia does well in translating the title as *The Music of Solitude* in English. Two solitudes come together, as it were, to sort out their relationship with time. They actually ask of themselves if they are merely whiling off time but then this perspective gets dispelled when they find themselves debating on fundamental existential questions regarding life and death. Very different from each other, they take a journey into self-reflexivity together. Two solitudes create a symphony and live together in harmony despite being so different!

The phenomenal person that she was, Krishna ji's life and story cannot be confined to a single article. Nor can one "sum up" here. Though she believed in "giving", she always kept back a lot, deep inside her, conserving her enormous vision and storehouse of memories to be churned out in her writing from time to time. Towards the end, she repeatedly said "Yaar, there isn't enough time." She passed away fully live with the urge to give more. Alas, the body cannot live up to the vision of such towering, larger-than-life personalities …

(First published in "Indian Literature", Sahitya Akademi's Bimonthly Journal, March-April 2019)

□□